D1057935

BASED ON A TRUE STORY, BY

Marie True Evans

—⚹—

Guinevere's
CHILD

outskirts press

Guinevere's Child
All Rights Reserved.
Copyright © 2019 Marie True Evans
v5.0

The opinions expressed in this manuscript are solely the opinions of the author and do not represent the opinions or thoughts of the publisher. The author has represented and warranted full ownership and/or legal right to publish all the materials in this book.

This book may not be reproduced, transmitted, or stored in whole or in part by any means, including graphic, electronic, or mechanical without the express written consent of the publisher except in the case of brief quotations embodied in critical articles and reviews.

Outskirts Press, Inc.
http://www.outskirtspress.com

Paperback ISBN: 978-1-9772-0202-4
Hardback ISBN: 978-1-9772-0203-1

Cover Image by Marie True Evans

Outskirts Press and the "OP" logo are trademarks belonging to Outskirts Press, Inc.

PRINTED IN THE UNITED STATES OF AMERICA

*This book is dedicated
to the memory of my mother
Mary*

So near to God am I
That if I stretch my hand
I feel it in his own
And firm in love I stand

No night of mine grows dark
No path of mine grows wild,
So near to God am I
His little child

Author unknown
(Handwritten among my Mother's papers)

Acknowledgements

With gratitude to:

Mel Layos, my editor, for his discerning eye

Kay Tuxford, my story/writer consultant, for her guidance and encouragement

Richard Lawrence True, my brother, who searched for the truth to what really happened

Cover photograph of Mary Jane Ellis Beeler

Chapter 1
1921—San Diego, California

One could not imagine such misery existed in such an idyllic setting. The weather was fair and glorious as it always was in San Diego. Days were warm, and evenings called for a light jacket; 'Perfect suit weather', the natives would boast.

Ocean Beach was a quiet seaside community of moderately priced family homes, mainly Craftsman bungalow styles; a working-class neighborhood where friendly neighbors looked out for each other. Many of the homes had avocado trees and fruit bearing trees growing in the yards. And roses were abundant in the gardens. When the breeze was right, the residents could smell the salt spray from the ocean nearby.

Guinevere Davies Dierks, a strikingly beautiful woman of thirty-five, and her five-year-old daughter Mary Jane, a pretty child with fair skin and golden red hair, walked hesitantly along the road. Despite her beauty, Guinevere appeared somewhat pale and wan. Although roughly gathered at the nape of her neck, wisps of her luxurious auburn hair were tossed about by the soft breeze. Her clothes, once fine, looked tired now. Gwen, as she was known by her family, held a bag in one hand and Mary Jane's hand in the other. Mary Jane held her doll.

The child's clothes were exquisite. Her dress was of sheer white cotton voile with lace trim at the hem and sleeve. She wore black leather Mary Janes with soft white cotton socks that folded with a ruffle just below the knee. The crisp white silk 'peau de soie' bow atop her head stood five inches tall. As they walked along, Gwen's long skirt brushed the child's legs.

They halted periodically, and Gwen would sigh, her demeanor solemn. It was the second time they had passed by the home at 4877 Muir Avenue, and the child had noticed that they seemed to be going in circles. She stopped and looked up at her mother, "We were already by here, Mama."

Gwen took a deep breath, "Yes, I know, Dear. Mama was just a little confused." When Mary Jane looked into her mother's eyes, she hugged her doll closer.

They approached the home, a modest, well-kept cottage of painted white stucco, surrounded by perfectly groomed flower beds and lawn. Gwen stepped onto the porch with Mary Jane. She bent down next to the child and spoke to her, shakily, "Mary Jane, dearest, these people want you to stay with them for a while."

The child looked puzzled. "Why?"

Gwen swallowed hard. "Well, they have always wanted a little girl. But, they don't have one of their own. And so, you have been invited to play."

Gwen straightened up and tried to keep her composure. She knocked.

The door was answered by Edith Beeler, a tall but portly woman in her late thirties, her demeanor reserved but pleasant. Her brown skirt and blouse were well made, but plain. Her reddish-brown hair was worn in an upsweep style with a knot atop her head. She looked down at the child. "Hello, Mary Jane." She bent slightly towards her, and when she did, Mary Jane recoiled. Edith Beeler had a musty smell about her person. "How nice that you have come to our home. We have some cookies and milk in the kitchen for you." She straightened again.

She spoke to Gwen, slightly sympathetic. "Thank you for bringing her."

Gwen felt her throat tighten. She handed the bag to Edith Beeler, then stooped and hugged Mary Jane to her, fighting back tears. "Have a nice time Mary Jane, dearest. And remember how much I love you."

Edith Beeler took Mary Jane by the hand and entered the house. Gwen turned and walked away. Mary Jane tried to look back at her Mama as Edith Beeler shut the door, cutting off her view.

Gwen was half-way down the block when her knees buckled, and she sat on the side of the road and buried her face in her hands. She sobbed as if her heart were broken... and indeed it was.

The interior of the Beeler's home perpetually smelled of furniture polish and cleaning fluids. The furnishings were formal and of good quality. In the living room, an oriental carpet covered the floor. The Victorian style sofa of carved mahogany was upholstered in maroon velvet, and the matching chairs were covered in blue tapestry. Lace doilies, antimacassars as they were known, covered the backs and arms of the furniture. All was in good order and everything in its proper place.

After milk and cookies, Mary Jane had gravitated to the piano and sat tapping on the keys. Edith Beeler had motioned to young Bert, the Beeler's eighteen-year-old son, to sit next to the child on the bench.

Bert was just under five foot ten inches tall and of medium build. He had brown unruly hair which he always fought to keep slicked down with pomade, but his passion for motorcycle riding made that difficult. He was a boy who loved being out-of-doors and resented having to go to school and then to work a job. A simple kid, without ambition to accomplish anything further than the next bike ride. Not a mean bone in his being, but neither did he have much in the way of a backbone. If there was a difficulty, he simply walked away rather than face a confrontation.

Mary Jane got up and walked over to the window and looked out. She turned and looked at Edith Beeler. "I want to go home now."

Edith came to the window and shut the curtains "This is your home now, Mary Jane."

The child responded emphatically. "No, I want to go home now to see my Mama and Eddie and Rosie."

Edith Beeler took the child's hand and walked her into the sunroom where her husband, Gilbert Beeler, an invalid, a mild-mannered man in his early forties, was confined to a daybed. She called to her son, "Come along, Bert!" Young Bert followed her to the sunroom.

"We are your family now, Mary Jane. I am your new mother, and this is your new father and Bert is your new brother. You don't have that other family any longer."

The child cried in disbelief. "No, no! I want my Mama and Eddie and Rosie! I want my Mama! I want my Mama!"

Edith spoke with an edge to her voice. "Mary Jane, you are our little girl now. You will call me Mother Beeler and you will call your new father Dad Beeler."

Mary Jane, now hysterical, screamed, "No, you're not my mama, you're not my mama!"

Bert started to speak. "Mother, maybe we should..."

Edith Beeler raised her hand and smacked Mary Jane so hard that she fell to the floor. Edith stood there, implacable, like a piece of stone. Mary Jane sobbed in disbelief and shock. Edith reached down and grabbed the child by the arm. Bert started to say something but thought better of it. She marched Mary Jane over to the desk and found the adoption papers where they lay. She turned to her and waved the papers and shook them in her face. "These papers say that that we are your new family, and that's the way it is! You are now Mary Jane Beeler. Do you understand me?"

Mary Jane answered between sobs. "Y-y-yes."

Edith Beeler's jaw relaxed a bit. "Fine! I will take you to your room." She took the child by the arm and walked her down the hallway.

Gilbert Beeler, dismayed, watched wordlessly. Young Bert shook his head in disapproval and left the house.

The child's small bedroom was wallpapered in a tiny pink floral pattern. There was a single bed with a ruffled bedspread and a handmade quilted coverlet. A child's dressing table and chair of white wicker were against one wall and a small bookcase and desk stood across the room. There was an oval hand-hooked rug of multi-colored cotton on the floor. The open window was draped with ruffled curtains of soft white eyelet that fluttered in the breeze. Mary Jane huddled in a corner of the room, crying. She hugged her doll.

In later years, she would recall that as 'the day all happiness ended'… the day she lost her Mama, brother, and sister.

Chapter 2
1923—Ocean Beach

Edith sent Mary Jane to the Baptist Sunday school, which was a bit tricky, because they disapproved of most things that were fun. For instance, they were dead set against card playing, a pastime Mary Jane occasionally enjoyed with Dad Beeler. But, she loved the Bible stories, and was fast in finding Bible verses she found meaningful, and she always 'spoke a piece' for programs.

Mary Jane knew that Gilbert was a kind man. Their relationship had grown to be a warm and caring one, but both understood that their affection for one another created resentment from Edith Beeler. So, they were careful to be quiet friends.

When Mary Jane came home from school, she would sit on the end of the daybed and go over her homework with Dad Beeler and share her impressions of the day. And he, in turn, would read to her the stories that he thought she would find interesting in the papers he collected.

One of her greatest pleasures was to roam the hillsides to gather bouquets of violets and shooting stars. The violets were not the usual purple, but they were yellow with little black centers and they were fragrant. It was easy to lose track of time, and she would often have to race home to do her household chores.

She was never allowed to ride a bicycle because she might hurt herself. Edith was adamant about that possibility. And Mary Jane was always warned to be careful. The child was perpetually in an anxious state regarding her activities.

One Saturday, seven-year-old Mary Jane entered the room, her dress torn, scrapes upon her knees and elbows, grease stains on her socks.

Gilbert looked up from his paper. "Mary Jane, whatever happened to you? Quick. Come over here." He grabbed a cloth on the side of the daybed and started to try to tidy her up, but he stopped his efforts when his wife entered the room.

Edith placed her hands on her hips when she saw the child. "Mary Jane! What have you done?"

Mary Jane's heart raced, and she felt panic rising in her throat. She shuddered, *Oh no, I'm gonna' get it this time.* She stammered, "I-I thought I might be late, so Brendan gave me a ride home on the handlebars of his bicycle. But then," she swallowed, "the wheels hit a rock in the road, and I tumbled off, and I'm so sorry."

Edith marched over to her and looked over her scrapes and bruises. "I've told you not to ride a bicycle. Just look at you! You're a mess!" Then she saw her torn and soiled dress. "And do you have any idea how long it took me to make this dress?"

Mary Jane cowered, "I'm sorry. I'm sorry."

Edith continued, "And I've told you before, that you have to look perfectly groomed at all times. Otherwise, what kind of mother will they think I am? But, you don't think about that, do you?"

She grabbed Mary Jane by the arm and marched her to the bedroom. The child began to cry. "I'll be better. I'll be better."

Edith taunted, "Boys can roll in the gutter and come up gold plated, but girls have to be perfect or they're punished! You'll stay in your room until I say you can come out. Maybe you'll think better of making a fool of yourself the next time."

Gilbert Beeler pleaded, "Mother, she didn't mean to have a fall. Please don't punish her."

Edith, now infuriated at being reprimanded, smacked Mary Jane, who started to cry. "Stop crying! Stop it now, or I'll really give you something to cry about!"

Gilbert shook his head, then picked up his Christian Science Monitor and started to read.

There never was any room for joy in her life. The child felt like a mechanical doll -- programmed at every turn. Never any freedom. No room for error. Never any forgiveness.

The next time she wore the dress, she looked down at the repair which was barely noticeable. She thought Mother Beeler was good at some things, but mostly she thought she was good at the beatings.

Chapter 3
Elementary School Years

Mary Jane attended school at the Ocean Beach Elementary School which was a welcome reprieve from home life. The school was originally built in 1909 and was only two rooms, but the community of Ocean Beach had grown greatly by 1921 when she had attended first grade. The school went from grades one through six, and several grades were taught at one time in each room.

They sang songs in the morning for the first half hour and then studied reading, writing and arithmetic, as well as geography and history. They practiced folk dancing, including some American Indian chants and dances. The teachers ran a tight ship. There was to be no tardiness, no gum chewing, no whispering or note passing. Despite the strictness, Mary Jane knew that she would rather be in school than at home.

Each day, she walked to and from school with her friend Jessie, who had been adopted by the Dunbar family. Jessie was a heavy-set girl of eight with lovely long curly brown hair. And when Emma Dunbar enrolled Jessie in dance class, Edith made sure that Mary Jane was also entered in the class. The girls were great friends and were delighted to have the time together.

It was seven blocks from her home to the school and along the way, for the first few years, the roads were a fine powdery brown sand, and in some spots, there were deep ruts after a rain and washout. Mary Jane was mindful of her steps and took care not to soil her shoes and socks. The streets, although tree-lined, were not yet paved, but most of the new homes along the way boasted lovely gardens. The girls didn't dawdle in the morning to make sure they arrived at school on time. But, Mary Jane loved flowers and on the way home, she would often stop to smell the roses which grew in great profusion.

They were never in a rush to get home; they loved their time together and the chance to commiserate about their miserable home lives. Jessie didn't have it so easy either at the Dunbar home. She told Mary Jane that her adoptive father beat her for the least little thing. She said that he was so mean, but that her new mother never did anything about it because she was afraid of him. So, Jessie said that she just tried to stay out of his way. Somehow the girls found humor as they compared notes about their lives, and they would giggle about things from time to time. They were grateful for each other's friendship.

Parents' Day had been scheduled at school. During recess, Mary Jane was playing kickball with the other children in the schoolyard. Gwen had stood watching from afar, hidden in a secluded spot behind a tree outside of the fenced yard. Mary Jane was being careful not to soil her dress.

Suddenly, the ball got away and rolled towards Gwen. Mary Jane chased the ball to the fence. She stopped, sensing her mother's perfume, but when she looked up, Gwen was gone. Memories flooded back of her mother and she was filled with a sense of longing, remembering the way she looked, the way she smelled and her loving touch. The feelings were so overwhelming that she had to stop and catch her breath, and the sense of loss was heard in her exhale.

She often dreamed of her mother and she would awaken crying. Each night she prayed that she would wake up and this life would disappear, and she would, once again, be at home with her family.

Later in the day, when Mary Jane and her classmates were seated at their desks, Edith Beeler entered with the other mothers. A girl at the desk next to Mary Jane leaned over and whispered, "Your mother just came into the room."

Mary Jane leaned over and whispered, "That's not my real mother. That's Mother Beeler, and she's mean as a snake. My real mother is beautiful."

Her friend whispered back, "Where is she?"

Mary Jane sighed, "I don't know. She got lost."

Chapter 4
Downtown San Diego

One summer day, on a corner in the shopping district of downtown San Diego, Edith carried on a flirtation with her friend Bob the plumber. Mary Jane remembered when he had come to the house to make repairs. He was a tall, gangly man in his mid-forties with jet black hair. Mary Jane, who waited impatiently, thought that he had funny black bushy eyebrows. She heard their somewhat muted conversation and she thought that Mother Beeler spoke much nicer to the man than she did to Dad Beeler.

Soon, Mary Jane tugged on Edith's skirt and whispered, "I have to go to the bathroom."

Edith hissed back, "Just hold it!" Then, continued her conversation.

The child fidgeted and shifted from one foot to the other. "Mother, please."

Edith ignored her and kept on with her conversation. Mary Jane felt like she would burst, but she held it until she couldn't stand it any longer, and then she lost control and wet her pants. She hung her head and whimpered. Bob heard the child moaning and noticed her distress. He motioned to Edith that there was a problem. Mary Jane was afraid to look up. She was mortified.

Edith looked down at Mary Jane and saw that her legs were dripping with urine and her socks were soaked. She gave Bob a pained smile. "I'm sorry, but I've got to go."

She grabbed Mary Jane by the arm, her face contorted with rage, and marched her across the street into Marston's

Department Store. As she walked through the store, there were occasional women who noticed the child's distress and shook their heads in disapproval.

Mary Jane cried, "I'm sorry, I'm sorry. Please, Mother Beeler. Please don't be mad at me."

Inside the department store ladies' room, she stripped off Mary Jane's urine-soaked underpants and held them over the child's face for so long, that Mary Jane had trouble drawing a breath. "There! Perhaps that will remind you not to wet your pants, and when I say to 'hold it', I mean hold it!"

When Edith released her hold, and the child finally got to take a breath, she cried loudly.

"Just shut your mouth and stop crying!"

The child cried through her sobs, "You're mean! You're mean! You're not my Mama!"

Edith smacked her. Mary Jane cried again. She put the child's panties back on, grabbed her hand and left the store.

The next week, while shopping at the fabric store, Edith searched for material and Mary Jane sat looking out the store window. The child's clothes were always beautiful as Edith was a very talented seamstress, but she was made to stand for hours on end while Edith fitted her for dresses which was just torture for her. If she wiggled, she got her legs smacked.

Today, Edith was shopping for a special material to make a party dress for Mary Jane. There was to be a mother/daughter tea given at the Ocean Beach Women's Club, and Edith wanted to make sure that Mary Jane's dress was the most beautiful there.

Suddenly, Mary Jane saw her mother, Gwen, walk out of a neighboring store with her brother, Eddie, now ten, and her sister, Rose, age six. It had been two years since she had seen her family. Gwen looked painfully thin and pale. And the children appeared quiet and subdued.

Mary Jane cried, "Oh, there's my Mama! There's my Mama and Eddie and Rosie!"

Edith spun around, glimpsing Gwen and the children. She grabbed Mary Jane as she tried to leave after them. Edith yanked her by the arm and shoved her into a chair in the corner of the store. "Just sit there until I'm finished shopping. Not one sound out of you or you will get it when we get home."

"But, I want to see them."

Patrons in the store turned to stare. Edith glowered at her.

Mary Jane dry sobbed as Gwen and the children slowly disappeared around a corner. Her feelings of elation plummeted into that of despair.

Back home at the Beeler's, Mary Jane was in her room. She thought about her Mama and she didn't remember that she was so thin. She tried to recall her voice, but it just kept slipping away. She thought about Eddie and Rosie and how they had grown since she last saw them. They weren't smiling, but they were still with her Mama. Then, the passing of time became a painful reality to Mary Jane.

She spoke to her doll as she played with her. "Don't you worry. I'll be a good Mama. I won't ever leave you." Then, she kissed and hugged the doll.

Chapter 5
Guinevere

Gwen's mother, Cora Josephine Smythe (nicknamed Daisy) married Owen Thomas Davis, and gave birth to two daughters, Guinevere and Constance.

Guinevere (Gwen, as she was called) was born in Berkeley, California, August of 1886. No firm records of her birth seem to have survived the great earthquake and fire of 1906, which destroyed most of what was recorded prior to that date in the San Francisco area. Gwen and her sister Constance (called Connie), who was four years younger, later took the Welsh form of their last name, Davies.

The girls' father, Owen Davis, was a world champion broadswordsman, a type of fencing competition, from Chester, England, a small town near Wales. Both his parents were Welsh. Davis fought under the British flag in South Africa before coming to America, where he became a Captain in the United States Army.

When Gwen was five and Connie was six months old, Daisy filed for divorce. Twice she left her husband and went to live with her mother. The first time was when Gwen was two years old. She claimed that, "he was a drunkard and had treated her 'in the most-cruel manner' and had physically assaulted her."

He must have sounded convincing in his apology and his promise of better times, because she moved back with him for a time. When Gwen would hear them arguing, she would run to her room and pray, "Please, make Mama and Daddy stop being mad. Please, make Mama and Daddy love each other." But finally, Daisy left for good.

Gwen lived in her grandmother's home in Berkeley, California with her mother and her younger sister for about a year. Her grandmother, Cora Agnes Bailey Smythe, was an English teacher in Berkeley. She became the first woman to teach English at The College of California that later became the University of California.

Gwen adored her grandmother. They were kindred spirits. Cora was a strong woman who knew her own mind, and where Gwen's mother could be manipulated, her grandmother held strong to her convictions.

Two years later, Daisy married Charles Farson, a successful businessman. They moved to a nearby home in Berkeley not far from the University. The house was a tall, dark grey Victorian style home; three stories, but narrow. Gwen told her mother that she didn't think the house looked very friendly.

Leaving her grandmother's home was a great sadness for Gwen, and she felt the loss keenly. No longer would she be able to sit each evening and read with her beloved grandmother, and then share her thoughts with one who understood her.

During the next twelve years of her marriage, Daisy gave birth to five more daughters. The family 'hearsay' was that the two families of daughters were not particularly close with each other.

Gwen resented that her step-father always seemed partial to his own daughters, and never was kindly towards her. Her sister Connie managed to get around him, but Gwen was always at odds with Charles Farson. She resented his strict rules and would taunt "You're not my real father; you can't tell me what to do!" She told her friends that her step-father hated and abused her, at one time dragging her down a long flight of stairs by the hair, after he had become enraged from drinking. She said she was made a 'slavey' around the house, a teen-age slang of the times, but that her mother, Daisy, was terrified of her husband, Charles, and would say nothing that might antagonize him.

Gwen was sent to St. Elizabeth's Convent School in Oakland where she was educated. She was a bright student, but she was always questioning the way things were done at school. "Must we do things that way?" or, "Why do we have to follow them?" and "Why can't we do things our own way?" One or two of the nuns were sympathetic to this beautiful, willful girl, but most were disapproving. Gwen could hardly wait for graduation day to come. Her mother would say, "Don't wish your life away... Live in the here and now."

"You've said it before, Mother dear, 'Patience has never been one of my virtues!'"

She was only sixteen years old when she married the first time to Dennis Toole, a tall, handsome man of twenty-eight. Gwen had found him a dashing figure. They were living in San Francisco, but the marriage lasted only three months before they divorced. Gwen said that she thought that he was rigid in his beliefs and was unwilling to see her side in any situation. She found him to be selfish and narrow minded and ungenerous of spirit, and not someone with whom she wanted to spend the rest of her life.

In December of that year, she married again to Roy Haines, a sailor on the USS Vicksburg at Mare Island, but that marriage lasted a short time, as well. She said that she became aware that he had a drinking problem and that did not sit well with her. It had become clear that he had no ambition whatsoever to accomplish anything in life. She had no patience with one who was lazy and slovenly. Once again, she filed for divorce.

This was all highly unusual in those years, and the two divorces were announced in the newspaper under the headline in the San Francisco Call, December 5, 1903: *Young Divorcee Marries and Divorces Again Within the Same Year.*

That Christmas holiday, Gwen and her mother were preparing a meal in the kitchen. "Consider your choices more carefully, Gwen. Your motto seems to be 'if a little's good, more's better'. Don't be such a glutton about life. Can't you just try to be more moderate?"

Miffed, Gwen replied, "None of my friends are so critical of me."

"Well, if you want to hear what you want to hear, ask your friends. But, if you want to hear the truth, ask your mother!"

"Times have changed, Mother!"

Her mother admonished her, "Perhaps times have changed, but men are still the same! If you must push too hard to make something happen, it's probably not the right thing."

"And what exactly does that mean, Mother?"

"You keep choosing partners that are not appropriate and then you insist on trying to make them fit into your world."

Gwen said, "Oh you just don't understand, Mother."

"Yes, I do understand. I was once your age. I know that you can have whatever you want in this life, but when you realize the cost to you is when you will determine how badly you want it."

Gwen wiped her hands on a cloth and turned and walked away.

Sadly, Daisy died of complications of childbirth one month after her seventh daughter was born. She was thirty-nine years old, and her eldest daughter, Gwen, was only eighteen.

Gwen hadn't realized the depth of her mother's devotion, nor the emptiness she would feel once she was gone. Where she used to argue a point and disagree with her mother's advice, now she was more thoughtful about her choices. She tried to think about what her mother would say and how she might feel when faced with a similar decision about life. She often regretted that she was not more mature while her mother was still alive. She wished she had been more loving towards her and had not taken her mother's love for granted.

Some years after her divorce from Roy Haines, Gwen's step-father introduced Gwen to his friend, Henry Dierks, an entre-preneurial businessman. Henry owned the Palm Garden Café in Vallejo and the Louvre Café in San Francisco. He also began investing in real estate in the Vallejo area, much of which was used as rental properties.

Henry was attractive and refined, although somewhat reserved. The first time they were together, Gwen told him all about herself... her life, her marriages, her mistakes. He listened and heard it all, but none of it mattered. He loved her. He thought she was wonderful just the way she was. He admired her courage and he loved the way she looked and everything about her; the way she made him feel when he was with her.

He asked her if she wanted children, and she said yes. She told him that even though she had helped her mother to raise six other girls, she could hardly pass a baby pram without stopping to look at the sweet child.

In Henry, Gwen saw a man she could depend upon – a good man. Even though she was not passionately in love with him, she felt that she could grow to love him, and she knew that she would have a good life with Henry.

There was something very seductive to Gwen about being

loved so totally and without reserve. She thought that she would finally be loved, in spite of all else, and for just the way she was, without having to change.

On December 7, 1909, Guinevere Haines, then twenty-three, married Henry Dierks, forty-one, in San Jose, Santa Clara County, California.

Gwen's sister, Connie, came to live with her and Henry for a time. Gwen was fiercely independent and there were difficulties in adjusting to life with Henry who was somewhat regimented. Gwen had found Henry's rules and regulations stifling and had told him so. Henry said that he would try to be aware. She said that Connie had been constantly siding with Henry, and that was creating a rift in the family life. After Henry and Gwen 'patched up their differences', Gwen thought it best that Connie find her own place. She did, however, continue to finance Connie's higher education.

Gwen gave birth to her first child, Hans Dierks, May 9, 1912. It was a difficult birth and resulted in the child having a form of cerebral palsy. He was called Hansie and Gwen lavished great love and care on him.

After Hansie was born, Henry seemed to be more critical of Gwen, second-guessing her every choice. She felt that he had become more controlling, which did not sit well with her, and she told him so. Even so, she felt that he continued to oversee and critique her every move and she began to feel stifled in her home life.

Chapter 6
Late 1912—Vallejo, California

Nestled in the rolling foothills, where the Carquinez Straits meet San Pablo Bay, is the city of Vallejo, California. In 1912, one could board a ferry to San Francisco, or an electric railroad car to Napa.

Eastern Georgia Street had become the address for Vallejo's professionals as doctors, lawyers and businessmen moved into the large well-situated homes. Many of the city's older neighborhoods grew up during this time. Western Georgia Street and the surrounding streets became Vallejo's downtown area.

The Dierks home on East Georgia Street was a charming, two story house with a welcoming wraparound front porch. The home was furnished comfortably in soft tones and was filled with sunshine.

Near the window, Henry Dierks concentrated on paperwork at his desk. He was working on a proposal to purchase a commercial property in Vallejo. Hansie, seven months old, was in his carriage in the window.

Gwen, then twenty-six, stood just inside the adjoining room. There was a wide archway between the two so visibility was clear between them. She wore a painter's smock over her clothes, which were quite fashionable. Her long brown fitted skirt was of fine wool gabardine and the cream silk blouse had a wide spread collar with a soft lacey cravat.

She held a paintbrush and touched up a landscape that she created in oil, then she stepped back to view her work. "I do so love wild flowers."

Henry, barely listening, spoke without looking up. "Maybe that's because you are one."

Gwen gave a wry smile. "Very clever, Henry."

She took off her smock and wiped the paint from her hands. She waved her arm to indicate the wall of books, "Henry, do you realize that we have an entire wall of fascinating books, and you have hardly read a single one!"

Henry spoke, still concentrating on his proposal. "The books that matter to this household are the ledgers of accounts."

Gwen rolled her eyes and shook her head, then walked over to the statue of Buddha which was on a pedestal in a corner of her art room. "For instance, I find this concept of Buddhism fascinating. It allows for us to call on the God within us, and not just pray to some elusive being floating around in the clouds."

Henry, still not looking up, retorted. "That sounds blasphemous to me."

Gwen sighed in resignation. "Of course, it would, Henry."

Henry mumbled. "I don't know why you insist upon keeping that statue."

She threw up her arms, "Open your mind, Henry, and find some things that bring you joy!"

He put the pen down and looked up. "I don't begrudge you having fun, but can you just be reasonable?"

She tossed her head. "Being reasonable means that you never get to do what you want."

Henry went back to his work. "There's more to life than just having a good time!"

Gwen rolled her eyes again and ignored the remark. She walked over to stand beside Henry. She leaned over and played with his hair. "I have an idea. I can pack a picnic basket. We could find a secluded spot and spread our blanket out on a hillside." She leaned over and spoke softly in his ear. "Maybe a jug of wine, a loaf of bread and thou beside me; a little romance away from prying eyes."

Henry took off his glasses, set them on the desk and rubbed his eyes, then turned to look at Gwen. "That all sounds lovely, Dear, but there is no way I can stop what I'm doing. I really must finish this proposal in time. So, perhaps another day."

Gwen straightened up, visibly resigned to the situation. She thought that Henry was turning into an old 'fuddy-duddy'. She walked over to the armoire and took out her jacket. She placed her hat on her head, wove in her hat pin and then walked over to Henry as she pulled on her gloves. "Henry, I am off to Mare Island to collect the rents. Hansie has had his lunch and is comfortable but do remember to pay attention to him while you work. It's so very lovely out today, you might want to take him for a walk. I'll be back later this afternoon."

She walked over to Hansie and kissed him goodbye.

Henry waved over his shoulder. "Bye, dear."

Chapter 7
Mare Island

In her carriage, Gwen raced along the beach roads, her hair blowing in the wind. This was indeed one of her favorite times. The carriage was pulled by a perfectly matched pair of white horses and they raced faster and faster as their mistress urged, her own heart beat racing to match theirs. She was free, and the feeling was intoxicating. She could throw off 'the ties that bind' and was beholden to no-one. As she went along, neighbors waved at the sight of the beautiful girl with the auburn hair flying along in wild abandon. She waved back. As the sun sparkled on the water, the salt spray filled her nostrils, and she was exhilarated by the speed and the feeling of freedom as she flew along the roads.

Mare Island was actually a peninsula in the city of Vallejo, bordered by the Napa River, about twenty-three miles northeast of San Francisco. Three miles long and one mile wide, it was purchased by the government in 1854 and became the first United States Naval Installation on the West Coast. Since that time, it had grown greatly and in 1912 it boasted two large drydocks and the most recent addition of an aircraft carrier.

There was a large Pacific Fleet Naval Base on Mare Island, and among the properties were cottages that were leased by the fleet officers as a kind of 'pied-a-terre' when home from sea duty. Henry Dierks had invested in several of the cottages to use as rental properties. Gwen thought that they were rather pleasing.

She liked the wraparound porches and she thought the second story balconies romantic.

She arrived at the cottage occupied by Lieutenant Commander Mark St. Clair Ellis and his wife Elizabeth.

Gwen alighted from her carriage. She straightened her clothes, replaced her hat, approached the door and knocked.

After a moment, the door was answered by Mark Ellis. Upon seeing Gwen, he stepped outside of the door and shut it behind him. Gwen secretly looked forward to this visit. The first time she met him, Mark had fallen all over himself to be amiable, and she knew that he found her attractive.

Mark bowed slightly while keeping his eyes on Gwen, "Good afternoon. How very nice to see you again, Madame Guinevere Dierks."

She nodded and smiled, charmed by him, "Please, that sounds so very formal. All my friends call me Gwen." Then she added coyly, "And it's nice to see you, too, Lieutenant Commander Mark St. Clair Ellis." She smiled, "I must say that I do think that yours is a most beautiful name."

Mark answered with a twinkle in his eye. "Do you have any idea how I look forward to paying my rent each week?" Then he looked past her at the horse drawn carriage. "And to one who drives a carriage drawn by a magnificent pair of white horses."

Gwen smiled. "Thank you. They are my pride and joy... And they run at the speed of lightning. They really are beautiful, aren't they?"

Mark looked back at Gwen. "Not nearly as beautiful as their mistress."

She felt her cheeks flush. "You flatter me, Sir."

Mark handed her an envelope containing the rent payment, but he continued to hold on to it, his eyes remained on her. "You know, we might make a more pleasurable event of collecting the rent." He finally let go of the envelope.

Gwen laughed and turned to leave. She tossed her next comment over her shoulder.

"Oh, I don't know. On my way 'to and fro', I get to race the horses along the beach roads. What could be better?"

Mark started to follow her, calling after her. "Do you ever get into the city?"

Gwen turned back. "Occasionally, why?"

"I find myself in San Francisco fairly often, and I wonder if we might meet for lunch sometime."

Gwen shook her head, "I don't think so."

Mark persisted. "It's just for lunch. And I, for one, would relish the opportunity to slip away for a while."

Gwen hesitated a moment. She questioned the wisdom of accepting such an offer. After all, she was married. How would it look? But, it seemed ridiculous to be so hesitant and fearful of what others might think. And in that instant, she dismissed her concern. "Well, I do have to go into San Francisco for a dress fitting next Wednesday."

He bowed slightly. "Well then, shall we say noon on Wednesday? I'll meet you in the lobby of The Palace Hotel."

Gwen brightened at the prospect. "I hear the Palace Hotel is lovely."

Mark concluded. "Good, then it's settled. I shall look forward to it."

Gwen turned and walked toward her carriage. Mark followed her. He took her hand and helped her onto her seat. "Safe journey. Until we meet again."

She smiled down at him. "Alright, then, goodbye."

She removed her hat. She snapped the reins and the horses took off. His eyes followed her.

Gwen thought that there was something exciting about having a harmless flirtation. Life was seeming so humdrum lately. All the way home, she was in high spirits. If she had any thoughts that questioned the wisdom of meeting another man in the city, she quickly dismissed them. After all, it was just for lunch.

Chapter 8
1923—The Piano

E ven in the midst of all that misery, something wonderful did happen for Mary Jane. Edith Beeler had a friend whose sister was a piano teacher.

Edith escorted Mary Jane, in her best dress, into the comfortable, although disarrayed, home of Lillian Hinkle Williams. Lillian was a pleasant looking woman in her late thirties. Her blonde hair was worn short and curled and she wore unusually thick glasses. She had one glass eye and one quarter vision in the other, still she was a very accomplished musician and an excellent piano teacher.

Mrs. Williams smiled warmly at Mary Jane. "How do you do, Mary Jane? I'm sure we'll get along famously." She turned to Edith Beeler, "We should be finished in about an hour."

Edith addressed Mary Jane, "Mind your manners!" Then she turned and walked out the door.

Mary Jane was nervous about wanting to make a good impression. She sat at the piano and pressed down on the keys. She smiled at the delightful sound. Mrs. Williams sat beside her, and the lesson began.

Lillian had three children of her own and she recognized Mary Jane's anxiety. She was a very intuitive and kindly woman and the child soon felt at ease and she did very well in her first lesson.

She could hardly wait each week for her next piano lesson. As she progressed in her lessons, Lillian would hear her playing a note and would call out from the kitchen, "Sharp that F, or flat that B." And one day, Mary Jane said, "How do you know to do that?" From that point on, Lillian gave her 'ear training' classes. After a time, Mary Jane could play anything she could hear, and she could transpose music to any key for accompaniment.

She adored Lillian Williams. Sometimes, when she sat next to her on the piano bench, Mary Jane would try to memorize the veins in her hands. In later years, she would say that Mrs. Williams was the nicest, smartest, and kindest woman she ever knew. There were times that she could recall the smell of her lipstick.

Playing the piano became her refuge, and she took to it as her second self. When she played no one could hurt her; she escaped into her own world. The praise she received from Lillian Williams encouraged her to give her very best effort, and no one needed to remind her to practice.

Mary Jane continued to play the piano. She was a gifted pianist and from the age of eight, whenever she performed, her concerts were written up in the newspapers. She was always hopeful that her mother would read about her and come to see her performance.

Edith Beeler was very proud of Mary Jane's musical talent and of her accomplishments. She saved every newspaper clipping and program in a scrapbook. Edith certainly enjoyed the accolades she received from the ladies in the Women's Club regarding how pleased she must be with the child she had adopted.

Edith had taught Mary Jane to sew and to knit, but the child used her piano practice to escape having to do anything that smacked of needlework.

'A Fancy Floral Fantasy' was to be presented in the newly built Strand Theatre. It was a benefit for the Baptists and starred the piano students of Lillian Hinkle Williams. When Mary Jane walked into the theatre, which seated several hundred, she was a bit nervous at the prospect of performing in front of such a large audience. And then she was anxious that her mother, Gwen, would read about her and come to see her in concert. Perhaps she would be in the audience tonight.

That evening at the concert, Mary Jane and her friend Jessie were on stage, each seated at a baby grand piano, playing a duet. Mary Jane had been distracted as she glanced out at the audience to see if her Mama might have come.

Jessie leaned towards Mary Jane and spoke in a loud whisper, "Where's the end, Mary Jane?"

Mary Jane whispered back, "We've gone past it!"

The audience heard the girls and chuckled. Edith Beeler's face darkened. Somehow, as they whispered back and forth, the girls found a way to end the piece. The audience laughed and applauded. But Mary Jane knew that there would be consequences.

Backstage, Edith grabbed Mary Jane by the arm. "All the money I spend on your piano lessons, and you embarrass me like this!" She smacked Mary Jane, "And no ice cream for you!"

Mary Jane was disappointed because she would miss having a 'black and white' soda (vanilla ice cream with chocolate sauce) at the Strand Sweet Shop next door. But, that paled when compared to her disappointment at not seeing her mother in the audience.

Later, when she gave concerts, she would receive baskets of flowers from fans. They would sit in the audience and cry. When they were brought to tears, she knew she was doing well, but if the concert wasn't perfect, she got beaten.

Mary Jane Ellis Beeler

Edith Beeler

Gilbert and Edith Beeler

Left to right—Mary Jane Beeler and Jessie Dunbar, two of the little pupils of Lillian Hinkle Williams, who last ight presented an interesting program at the Thearle studios.

Lillian Hinkle Williams presented primary and intermediate grade dents in a recital last evening s o'clock at the Thearle studios. more advanced students will ear two weeks later, April 21, the same place.

he program Saturday evening e the public a glimpse of the ular every-day work in her dio. Mrs. Williams studied the ning system for beginners with e Dunning herself some years in New York City. Since com- here she has reviewed that rk with the Normal teacher of district, Miss Cara Garrett, and recently been in Los Angeles personal touch with Mrs. Dun- again. The psychology of the d mind is of special interest to s. Williams. Master Richard ler, the well known child violin pupil of Fred Lewis Hakel of Mission Hills School of Music, sted in the program, which was ented by the following mem- of the class:

elen Wetzel, Norma Williams ry Jane Beeler, Virginia Dall dia Chambers, Gladys Nichols e Reid, Loraine Garnett, Cath-erine Garnett, Jessie Dunbar, Dru-cilla Glasson, Elizabeth Case, David Ryan, jr., Dorothy Anne Carleton, Winnefred Varney, Doris Richards, Dorothy Wright, Kathryn Hellbron, Virginia Burch, Donald Ryan, Mary Oliver, Francis Oliver, Dorothy Hale, Rena Case, Mary Elizabeth Carleton, Irene Askins.

Lillian Hinkle Williams will present her nine year old pupil, Mary Jane Beeler, daughter of Mr. and Mrs. G. L. Beeler of Ocean Beach in a juvenile piano recital and tea Sunday afternoon at four at the residence of Mr. and Mrs. L. M. Lyons, 3154 Laurel street. Burlingame. Gloria Williams, will play violin numbers, with Rena Case as accompanist. Mrs. Rich-ard P. McCall, Mrs. D. N. Car-michael and Mrs. Elsie Ballantyne will assist at the tea table.

Mary Jane Beeler, aged 9, daughter of Mr. and Mrs. G Beeler of Ocean Beach, will entertain with a piano recital Musicale-tea to be given this afternoon by Mrs. Leonard Lyons.

Little Miss Mary Jane Beeler, daughter of Mr. and Mrs. O. L. Beeler of Ocean Beach, will be the central figure of an attractive musical-tea to be given at the home of Mrs. Leonard M. Lyons, 3154 Laurel street, Burlingame, this afternoon at 4 o'clock.

Mary Jane will present a piano re-cital, and will be assisted on the pro-gram by Gloria Williams, in a group of violin numbers, accompanied by Rena Case. This will be a juvenile program of great interest to those in-terested in student recitals.

Assisting at tea will be Mrs. D. N. Carmichael, Mrs. Richard P. McC and Mrs. Elsie Ballantyne.

The musical program in full fo lows:

Sonata in C Major, Allegro (M zart).

Invention No. 8 F Major (Bach). Romance in G Major (Spindle left hand only, Mary Jane Beeler. Concerto Op. 21 (Hungarian) (Ret ing), Gloria Williams, Rena Case the piano.

To a Wild Rose (MacDowell), Eas ern Dance (Torjussen), At Sunri (Homer Grunn), Tarrentelle in Minor (Risher), Mary Jane Beeler

Mary Jane and Jessie

Lillian Hinkle Williams

Chapter 9
1926—Ocean Beach

Mary Jane, age nine, sat practicing the piano, her red hair fashioned into corkscrew curls in the style of the day.

Edith Beeler walked over to Mary Jane who stopped playing upon hearing the footsteps. She turned towards her, a degree of fear on her face. Edith held an envelope. "Mary Jane, I have received word that your mother is in the hospital, gravely ill."

"Will she be okay?"

"I don't know that."

Mary Jane tried to hold back her tears, frozen. "Can you take me to see her?"

"No, that won't be possible." She saw the stricken look on the child's face and her demeanor softened. She looked at the letter in hand. "Why don't you sit and write her a letter?" Edith turned and left the room.

Shaken, Mary Jane walked to her room and sat at her desk. She was absolutely devastated; she felt like she was stone. She was totally traumatized as she thought about writing that letter to her beloved mother, Gwen. Slowly, she gathered stationery and envelope and put pen in hand. She wished she had a better hand writing, but she was left handed and her teachers and Mother Beeler had all insisted that she write with her right hand.

She wanted to tell her Mama of her extreme unhappiness, but she didn't dare, because Mother Beeler would read the letter and she would suffer for it. Her pen hovered over the stationery, as she contemplated her words.

She thought, *Mama, why did you leave me here? Why did you abandon me? I'm so dreadfully unhappy. I long to see you and Rosie and Eddie. Please get well and come for me.*

She finally began her letter:

Dear Mama,

I am so sorry that you are sick in the hospital. I am in fourth grade now and I am getting A's in geography and history, but I have trouble in arithmetic. I am learning to play the piano. I hope you get well soon so that you can come to my recital next month. You can bring Eddie and Rosie, too.

Love,
Mary Jane

Later, in her room, Mary Jane, under the covers, hugged her doll. Tears stained her cheeks. She folded her hands and prayed quietly. She slept fitfully and lay awake much of the night wondering if her Mama would get the letter.

Over the next few days she worried, but there was no word from Mother Beeler about the letter. Finally, Mary Jane walked up to her as she worked at her desk. Edith spoke without looking up, "Well, what is it?"

"Did she get my letter?"

Edith stopped her writing and looked up. "I don't know. But, I am very sorry to tell you that she has passed away."

Mary Jane spoke hesitantly, "Is she dead?"

"Yes, she is."

After a moment, Edith went back to her work. Mary Jane, overcome with sadness, walked away.

All hope of being reunited with her family was shattered and she was filled with despair. She lost her appetite, and she couldn't sleep. Some time after her mother died and she knew that her brother and sister were lost to her, Mary Jane became quite ill. As she lay in bed with a fever, Edith sat beside her and bathed her body with cool cloths.

Delirious, Mary Jane looked up at Mother Beeler and called out, "Mama!"

Edith visibly softened, then she stood and left the room to get a fresh cloth.

Mary Jane turned her head towards the door and saw a bright light. She got up and went to the door, opened it and stepped out onto the porch. Outlined in the bright light was a vision of her mother, Gwen. After a moment's hesitation, she walked out onto the lawn.

The vision never looked directly at Mary Jane and spoke void of emotion. "There are only a few times in life that you can be happy. You can choose to have your happiness now or when you are older."

Mary Jane contemplated. She thought about how she wasn't happy now, and maybe she could look forward to happier times. "Well, I guess I'd like to have my happiness when I'm older. But, Mama, why did you leave me? What did I do wrong? I don't understand. Why didn't you want me anymore?" She started to cry.

The vision spoke, "Everything will be alright. You'll be okay," and then the vision disappeared.

Mary Jane sank to her knees, covered her face and sobbed. "That's all," she cried, "no apology, no explanation for what happened?"

Edith came outside on the lawn to Mary Jane. "You have to come back inside, Mary Jane. You're very ill. Come back to bed."

Mary Jane was sobbing, "Mama, Mama!" She gathered the child, tenderly, and carried her back inside. Edith Beeler was an excellent caregiver and she did nurse Mary Jane back to good health.

When Mary Jane spoke of the vision, and others questioned its reality, she swore it was true, that it really happened.

It was late 1926, and Mary Jane and Jessie walked home from school together as usual. "Jessie, do you remember your real mother?"

Jessie answered, "Yes. I remember her, but she was mean to me. She loved her horses, and she was very kind to them, but she whipped me every chance she got. She said she never really wanted children, so I guess she was glad to be rid of me, and she let me be adopted. But I don't think I'm any better off now."

Mary Jane sighed, "My real mother wasn't mean at all. She never hit us. She was really nice, and I think she loved us a lot." She turned to Jessie. "I saw my Mama one time before she died, but she didn't see me. She was with Rosie and Eddie. They were both still with my Mama. Why would she let me be adopted? Why would she do that?"

Jessie shrugged her shoulders. "Maybe she had too many children."

They walked along in silence for a few moments. Then Mary stopped and turned to Jessie. "One day when I was out in the backyard picking lemons from the trees, Mother Beeler called to me saying, 'Your father is here.' So, I dropped my basket and ran into the house. But when I came into the room, there was a crippled old man with a twisted face. Then I screamed, 'He's not my father, he's not my father'. And I ran out of there. And then after he left, I got another whipping."

"Well, who was it?

"I don't know. It wasn't my father. I remember my father." Again, they walked along in silence.

After a few moments, Mary Jane turned to Jessie, "I wish I could live with Mrs. Williams. Don't you?"

"Yeah, that would be great."

"Oh, Jessie, guess what! I learned three pages of the new music?"

Jessie smirked, "Well that's nice, but I learned four."

The girls continued to play duets together. They were great friends, and the competition was fun. The friendship made life bearable for both girls.

When Jessie was fifteen, her family moved to Long Beach, where the Dunbars opened a roller-skating rink. Mary Jane felt that she was losing her dearest friend, but they remained friends for life.

After Jessie moved away, Mary Jane kept up with her music and dance lessons. She joined the Silvergate Girls Swimming Club. One of her teammates was Florence Chadwick. Through the years, she would laugh at herself for floating on a tire tube, while Florence swam the English Channel.

Chapter 10
1912—San Francisco

After much deliberation, Gwen decided to meet Mark as planned. She had been back and forth with what if's... What if a friend would see her? How would she explain the meeting without raising an eyebrow? But in the end, she dismissed them as ridiculous concerns. It was simply meeting a new friend for lunch.

That Wednesday, she decided to take the Southern Pacific train into the city and then catch a carriage to the hotel. The train would leave Vallejo at 10:15 a.m. and get her into San Francisco at 11:30 a.m.

Driving a carriage through the streets of San Francisco was like tackling an obstacle course. There were distractions in all directions. Coming down Market Street to Montgomery was in the very busiest area of the city. It was teeming with all manner of transportation. There were streetcars, horse drawn carriages, automobiles and wagons pulled by drays that were used by the merchants for supplies. The wide streets were lined with streetcar tracks and cobble stones between and there were wide flat areas of the road along the sidewalks.

There was not a man, woman, nor child that did not wear a hat, and for the women, the 'more grand', the better. The men were in suits and coats and the women wore long skirts and jackets, and all hustled back and forth across the street with no apparent guidelines as to when to cross and when to stop. The city was alive with horns honking, bells clanging, and people shouting and rushing in wild abandon in all directions.

She arrived at the interior courtyard of the Palace Hotel and then walked to the lobby where Mark was waiting. As he greeted her, he handed her a rose. She smiled up at him. "It's so very beautiful here. If there's time, do you think we might walk through the hotel before lunch?"

Mark, nodded, "Of course."

She inhaled the fragrance from the rose, "And thank you for my beautiful rose."

He bowed his head slightly, "Beautiful, but not as beautiful as you, Gwen."

She smiled at the flattery.

They walked through the gleaming marble lobby to the Palm Court. She stopped along the way to admire the surroundings. Reopened in 1909 after the devasting earthquake and fire of previous years, The Palm Court was San Francisco's most prestigious hotel dining room.

They entered the dining room and the maître d' showed them to their seats.

Gwen looked around the room and smiled.

The lofty iridescent glass ceiling, through which the sunlight filtered down in an amber flood, was further enhanced by numerous crystal chandeliers that hung throughout the room. The wood work throughout was old ivory-toned and there were lattice frames that were graced by palms throughout the room, which offered a bit of privacy for the diners.

Gwen said that she thought that the dining room was elegant. And he said that he was pleased that she found it so.

Mark asked if she would enjoy a glass of wine. And she answered that she thought that would be lovely.

He asked, "Would you prefer red or white?"

"White would be my preference."

Mark said that he would join her and ordered a bottle of La Terre Chardonnay." The waiter arrived and opened the bottle, then poured two glasses.

Mark raised his glass, and Gwen raised her glass, as well. "To friendship."

Gwen replied, "To friendship."

They clinked glasses and sipped their wine.

Conversation came easily for them. She asked about his life and how he came to choose a career in the Navy.

Mark told her that he had attended the University of Arkansas for three years, then received an appointment from his State Senator to attend the United States Naval Academy. After graduating in 1896, he had served aboard various ships and was made Lieutenant Commander in 1909.

He spoke about his current position as Magazine Officer at Mare Island Navy Yard and that his time there was drawing to a close. He said that he felt that he had accomplished much since he had taken the position. He had received praise from the community for keeping many of the citizens steady at work building a number of substantial buildings at the magazine; those of which greatly added to the safety of the area. Mark said that he was next to report aboard the cruiser Maryland in early November.

She asked how long he would be gone. He told her that the time would vary, but as a career Navy man, he would spend most of his time at sea.

She replied, "And what do you do when you are on land?"

He spoke about his invention, The Ellis Self Scoring Target, which had been patented and had become thoroughly successful. She asked him to tell her about the invention and he spoke about an article in *Our Navy Magazine*. He said that they asked him, "Why should enlisted men of the Navy be interested in your Self Scoring Target and of what benefit will it be to them?"

And he stated that, "my target will save the sailorman's life – will save work and will teach him to shoot."

He told her that they noted, that upon investigation, they found all three statements to be correct.

Gwen said that she was very impressed and that he must be so proud. He thanked her and asked her about herself.

She told him that she was presently managing several rental properties in the Vallejo area. She said that she came from a large family and that she was helping to educate her younger sisters. And as well, she continued her own education by taking various courses that were of interest to her. And lately, she had been studying art. And, of course, she was kept busy running a household and caring for her young child.

Mark told her that it sounded as though she had a full and rewarding life.

Gwen smiled, then became more serious. "So, tell me, Mark. How long have you been married?"

Mark had been heard to comment that he never could resist the touch of a woman's skin. But, he had also realized the importance of marrying well. At age thirty, in November of 1903, he had married Mrs. Elizabeth Tilghman, a socialite from Greenwich, Connecticut.

Mark's demeanor became more solemn. "I've been married to Elizabeth for nine years, most of which have been very difficult as she contracted Bright's disease not long into our marriage. I'm afraid that she has been an invalid for some time now."

His words gave her pause and Gwen suddenly felt uncomfortable at hearing that Mark's wife was an invalid. Somehow it didn't seem right for her to be sharing such a pleasant interlude with a man whose wife was suffering at home. She replied with sympathy, "How very difficult that must be for both you and her."

Mark sensed her discomfort. Then, he spoke sincerely, "Actually, Elizabeth and I no longer have the relationship we once had. We now share our home as brother and sister. Although I sympathize with her situation, it's been very disappointing for me." He looked over at Gwen. "You see, the desire of my life has always been to have children, a privilege denied me in my own home."

Gwen answered, "I am so sorry. I should think you would make a terrific father." Mark nodded in gratitude.

After a moment, he asked, "And how is married life treating you, Gwen?"

Gwen was thoughtful for a moment. She twirled the rose in her fingers, then lay it on the table. "My husband, Henry, is a good man, a good provider, and quite dependable. We have one child, Hansie, who is somewhat limited due to a difficult birth process." She smiled up at Mark, "But, he is beautiful and dear, and Henry is good with the child."

Mark replied, "I see."

The conversation continued in a pleasant manner. They spoke about family and their interests in life. They found that they shared much in common as to their intellectual interests. Questions about religious beliefs led into a more in-depth conversation regarding conventional church experience. Gwen said that she didn't hold much with the edicts of formalized religion, but that she was more spiritual about her beliefs. She had found the concepts of the spirit of God, as outlined by the Buddhists, most intriguing. Mark told her that he, also, had been intrigued by and interested in the practice of Buddhism for several years.

The luncheon ended with an invitation from Mark to meet again since this had been such a pleasant interlude. And that it had done his heart good to be out and about socially in the company of one so charming. It was, after all, difficult to be care-free and happy at home. No harm done, and would she please consider meeting him again for lunch when next she found herself in San Francisco. If she hesitated a moment, any notion of caution faded with the last sip of wine.

Gwen arrived home late afternoon, still titillated by the events of the day. Henry was working at his desk, as usual. He barely looked up as he greeted her, "Oh hello, dear. Did you have a nice day?"

Dinner with Henry that evening seemed so flat and mundane. It paled in comparison when she thought about her day in San Francisco. Her reality certainly could not compete with the glamour of her time with Mark. But then again, that had not been her reality.

Chapter 11
Early 1913—Gwen and Mark

Gwen and Mark met often in San Francisco. She found him charming, accomplished and interesting. The lure of romance was impossible for her to resist, and he became more and more important to her.

She arrived at The Palace Hotel, alighted from the carriage and paid the driver. Then, filled with anticipation, she turned and entered the hotel lobby and walked through to the Palm Court Dining Room. When she arrived, she spoke with the maître d' who showed her to the table that Mark occupied. Mark stood while she was being seated.

He addressed the maître d', "Thank you." Then, he turned to Gwen. "Wonderful to see you, as always. "

Gwen sat, and as she took off her gloves, she noticed a gift box of French perfume at her place. "And what is this?"

"It's a French perfume called "Heure Bleue" by the perfumier Guerlain. It means 'The Blue Hour.' Supposedly, that hour at dusk is when the flowers are at their most fragrant."

Gwen, delighted, replied, "How divine! Thank you. I love surprises."

Mark nodded, "One as lovely as you should always be surrounded by beauty."

She smiled, "I shall wear it when we next meet." She tucked the perfume in her purse, then looked around the room.

"This is truly a lovely hotel. I always find this dining room enchanting."

Mark replied, "Yes, it is a favorite of mine, too. But, more so when you are in the room."

She couldn't help but smile at the flattery. She knew she was beguiled, but the feeling was intoxicating. If there was a wee small voice that warned of temptation, she dismissed it as ridiculous to worry over. After all nothing had happened. It was just a flirtation. No harm done, and it made her feel alive.

Mark ordered champagne. The waiter arrived, uncorked the champagne and poured the two glasses. Mark nodded to dismiss the waiter, then raised his glass of champagne and proposed a toast. "To friendship and love."

They clinked glasses. Gwen smiled. They sipped their champagne.

"I've always meant to ask you, is St. Clair a family name?"

Mark replied, "It is now. I was born in St. Clair County, Missouri. My parents lived there in their early married life. Hence my middle name... of which I am most proud, by the way."

Gwen tilted her head to the side, "I never use my middle name. I was always teased in school."

Mark was quizzical, "Really?"

Gwen leaned forward as if to share a secret. "Shall I tell you what it is?"

Mark replied, "Please do."

She whispered, "It's Zepherina." She sat back, "But, I usually sign only my middle initial. In the Greek language it means 'a light breeze'. I always thought that sounded lovely."

Mark spoke with a twinkle in his eye, "To my way of thinking, that description sounds much too tame for you."

Gwen blushed, then asked, "And what about your family?"

Mark set his glass on the table. "My mother died when I was only four and my three brothers and I were raised by my grandmother. I always felt that my childhood was rather bereft of feminine tenderness, except for her." He looked at her beseechingly and spoke tongue-in-cheek. "So, you can see that I am in need of love."

Gwen laughed and then spoke in earnest, "Sad about losing your mother at such a young age. My own mother died when I was just eighteen, and that was very difficult for me. There were many times through the years that I could have used her wise counsel."

Mark asked, "And what would she have said about me?"

Gwen replied, pointedly, "Oh, no doubt... 'Stay away, Dear'!"

Mark threw his head back and laughed.

Then she smiled and sipped her champagne. Changing the subject, she asked, "What was life like growing up in Arkansas?"

Mark told her that the family moved to Arkansas in 1886. He said that both his father and his grandfather were much pleased with that part of the Country. His father found a farm of one hundred twenty acres, a quarter mile from his grandfather's farm. Being an industrious young man, he said that he worked on both farms. He remembered that he and his father hauled a number of wagonloads of lumber from the Van Winkle Mill that went into the building of the University of Arkansas.

Mark said that after they had been in Arkansas for a few years, his father took the family back to Missouri where they had left a number of household articles with some of their friends before leaving for their new home.

The trip was difficult. He said that they rode in a two-horse wagon with wooden spindles. A bucket of coal tar had been hung from the coupling pole and was used to lubricate the axles of the wagon. He remembered that the trip to Missouri was made after the Civil War, and as they went to and fro', they passed the battlefield of Pea Ridge. They could still see the fragments of the trees, and parts of the blue coats with brass buttons scattered over the ground. He told her that even though they were young, the vision had a sobering effect on him and his brothers, and his eyes were opened to the tragedies of war.

He seemed deep in thought for a moment.

Gwen reached out and touched his hand. "What a sad sight to witness at such a young age."

He answered, "Yes, it was."

That spring, on a beautiful day, Mark and Gwen lounged on a blanket and shared wine and sandwiches. The sky was an amazing shade of azure and the weather was glorious. The sun shone brightly, but they were comfortable in the shade of an old oak tree.

Gwen viewed the countryside. She was filled with a sense of pleasure, perhaps the feeling of being at one with nature. "I always think of these days as a gift from God." As she looked around she continued, "This vista is amazingly beautiful. I wish I had my easel and brushes."

Mark replied, "Spoken like a true artist."

Gwen blushed at his acknowledgement. "Yes, I manage to lose myself in my painting. Mostly landscapes and some still life in oil."

He was thoughtful for a moment. "And from what reality are you escaping?"

Gwen became wistful. "I'm afraid that Henry and I are two people who view life quite differently. Henry would, no doubt, be perfect for someone else, but I am feeling rather unfulfilled in this marriage." She looked down. "I guess I don't make a very good martyr because I have considered leaving him."

Empathetically, Mark replied, "As to martyrdom, in that I concur."

Mark filled Gwen's wine glass. "I certainly married with high hopes, as well. But, life doesn't always turn out as one planned. I've tried to make the best of a difficult situation. But, I can't deny myself all the pleasures of life." Gwen looked up. Mark smiled at her. "It goes against my nature."

She felt her cheeks flush, and she started to turn away, but he pulled her towards him. "I love you, Gwen." Then he leaned over and kissed her.

She felt that she had never known a kiss could be that compelling. All that day and evening, she would brush her hand on her lips to recall the feel of his mouth on her own.

The following week, Gwen sat at the kitchen table and poured tea for herself and her sister Connie, who stood pacing the floor. Although an attractive young woman, she was not beautiful like Gwen.

Connie stopped and shook her finger at Gwen, "You've always been a thrill seeker! It's like the time you told me that you planned to jump with a parachute from a plane over San Diego for the thrill of it."

Gwen laughed. "I was told that it was perfectly safe! No need to be anxious."

"Ha! And I told you that if anything happened to you, I would not be responsible for Hansie, and that you best think better of it before you considered throwing caution to the wind! So, you didn't go."

Gwen answered disgruntled, "Alright, alright, I remember. What a 'spoil-sport' you are! Sit and have some tea."

Connie sat at the table but continued, "And this dalliance of yours. You finally have a stable marriage, and a husband who adores you above all else. You have a wonderful life. Why would you want to put it all in jeopardy?"

Gwen sighed, "I didn't plan on it. It just happened. I've fallen in love with Mark." She sipped her tea.

Connie spoke in earnest, "But, your husband is such a nice man."

Gwen felt exasperated. "Yes, he is a very nice man, but he is so straight-laced and rigid. Sometimes I just want to scream!"

She leaned in to Connie. "With Henry, it was always the same thing, in the same way, in the same place, every time. And, she adds, I can't stand to kiss him anymore."

Connie shook her head, "All days aren't Sundays, Gwen. I do hope you will reconsider this path you are taking. No good will come of it."

Gwen felt deflated. She had thought that Connie would be more empathetic. "I have thought about it, over and over again. I do care about Henry and I suffer anxiety at the thought of hurting him. He is always so kind. And then, there is Hansie to consider. Henry so loves the child. Oh, I don't know. I have much to think about. The thought of living without Mark in my life is too sad, but I know I that I have more than just my own life to consider in making this decision. At this point, I'm not sure what I will do."

Chapter 12
The Beelers

Edith Lola Worley was born May 10, 1883 in a rural town in Oregon. Her father had walked out on her mother, leaving her with three children, two boys and a girl. Her mother liked the boys but never cared for Edith, who tried as she might, could never please her. She was always ridiculed if she failed to do all her work perfectly. If she peeled potatoes and her mother didn't feel that they were peeled close enough, she was made to peel the peels.

Her mother never approved of her daughter Edith, and made it known on more than one occasion that she wished that Edith had never been born. She seemed to look for reasons to beat Edith and to punish her for the slightest error in performance of her daily responsibilities. Somehow, she found Edith's presence a constant reminder of how her own life had turned out badly; she resented that life still offered the possibility of freedom and happiness for Edith.

As a young woman, Edith dated Gilbert Lawrence Beeler for a time, and he often proposed marriage, but she thought of him as more of a friend than a lover.

When Edith was twenty-two, she fell madly in love with a young man who came to work on one of the farms in the area. They dated for a time, and he became 'her everything', and before long, they became intimate. But, as soon as he found out that she was pregnant, he left her and told her that he had no use for a wife and family. Devastated, Edith vowed never again to allow herself to be that vulnerable.

When Gilbert learned of her predicament, he came to see her. He told her that he had always loved her and would be pleased to marry her and give the child his name. Relieved that she could escape the wrath of her mother, she accepted his proposal. But the betrayal of her lover and the years of abuse she had suffered at the hands of her mother left her bitterly disappointed and resentful of her lot in life. It was as if a shroud had settled and covered her soul.

They married and moved to Nebraska for a time, where Gilbert worked for a friend doing construction until he lost two fingers cutting lumber. Then, there was talk that work could be found with the railroad in California, so Edith and Gilbert moved the family to San Diego.

By 1910, there were one hundred homes in the community of Ocean Beach, which had been made livable with city water, gas and electricity, and a substantial streetcar line.

They bought a cottage on Muir Avenue, and in the first years of Prohibition, Gilbert ran a still out of the back yard, a practice that was common during those years. He was very resourceful and opened tobacco shops with gambling rooms in the back of the store. Gilbert was frugal and kept his eye out for a property that could be had at a good price. In this way, he purchased a few homes in the area to be used as rental properties.

Gilbert worked for the Santa Fe Railroad as a brakeman until his legs were crushed between two cars that became loose. Ever after, he was confined to a wheelchair. Fortunately, the household was able to survive on the income from the tobacco shops, the gambling houses and the rental properties. When, during the difficult times of the Depression, the tenants were unable to pay their rents, the Beelers trimmed the family budget and made do with whatever was available to them, but they did not evict their tenants.

Gilbert had always enjoyed the out-of-doors and after the accident, he would do what he could to help with trimming the low-lying garden areas. But, whenever they went out it was Edith who drove their Oldsmobile RIO car with young Bert riding in the rumble seat.

Edith learned to do anything a man could do around the house. From her work on the farm, she could repair anything that was broken, and put on a new roof if needed. She was an excellent cook and made most of her clothes, which were beautiful and fashionable. She took good care of Gilbert, even though she always managed to find fault with anything he ever did. He accepted his lot in life and was grateful for her care.

Gilbert had been a fairly attractive young man of slim build and one who had enjoyed playing sports. Now that he was no longer ambulatory, his feeling of freedom came vicariously through the books he read.

Through his studies, he had also become a Christian Scientist, a religion which emphasized divine healing as practiced by Jesus Christ. He was a member of the congregation of the Christian Scientist Church which was first organized in 1923 by four or five members. They met several places, including the Grace Apartments until, in 1930, they had their own building at Cable and Santa Monica Streets. He read the Christian Science Monitor daily.

Edith had social ambitions and joined the lady's society, The Ocean Beach Women's Club. Being accepted by the ladies of the community was very important to Edith. They met in their clubroom on Abbott Street in the wide end of the Flatiron Building. Edith was a member of the garden committee that was responsible for planting oleanders all along Brighton and Cable Streets, jacarandas on Defoe, hibiscus on Long Branch and acacias on Muir Ave. The Women's Club afforded Edith the socialization she craved. She enjoyed the camaraderie of women, and the accolades she received for her cooking and needlework projects.

When her friend Emma Dunbar, with whom Edith was highly competitive, adopted a little girl, Edith, not to be outdone, decided to adopt a child, as well. She would adopt a little girl and mold her into the perfect child. She had to be perfect in every way, and Edith would make sure of it, so as to reflect favorably upon her parenting skills. While Edith could never forgive her own mother's disdain of her, she would deign to prove herself to be a far better mother, and the child would be the proof of her success.

Chapter 13

1930—Ocean Beach

Edith Beeler often talked over the fence to her neighbor, Flora, a woman of Spanish descent who was in her mid-fifties. They were members of the same garden club; it was important to Flora to ingratiate herself with Edith as it was Edith who would judge the floral entries in the garden club events.

Edith spoke with a sigh, "I used to love to go dancing but, that all ended when my husband had his accident. It was all such a terrible mistake. He just looked away for an instant. Then you find your whole life changed, forever."

Flora spoke quietly, "You surely do have it rough, what with looking after your husband and raising a child without any help. I certainly do admire you."

Edith sighed, "Yes, I try very hard to be a good mother. It's been a comfort to have Mary Jane here, otherwise I'd be..." She paused a moment. "You would tell me if there was anything you think I should be aware of, wouldn't you?"

Flora hesitated before speaking again. "I do think you ought to know that your daughter has been asking me for help in finding her brother and sister."

Edith's demeanor stiffened. "Thank you for letting me know."

In her bedroom, Mary Jane was on her bed, propped up on pillows, reading a book. She had turned fourteen and was now called Mary by her friends.

She was never allowed to talk about her mother, Gwen, nor

her brother and sister. If Edith had an inkling that Mary was searching for them, she would go through everything of hers, looking for notes.

Edith walked into the room. She stood stiffly and waved a letter in front of Mary's face, "After all I've done for you, you go behind my back. Remember, I took you in when no one wanted you."

Mary was silent.

She continued, "Why ever would you want to try to find your family? You come from trash and you'll go back to trash!" She tore the letter up and marched out of the room.

Mary held her tongue. She was used to those harsh words. Anytime she asserted herself, Edith would lambaste her and try to degrade her and her family. But Mary knew that Mother Beeler's cruel words couldn't be true, because she remembered the beautiful, kind woman that once was her mother.

Through the years, Mary kept asking questions about her family whenever she felt safe in making the inquiry. Arlene Schroeder was a girlfriend from school, and she had told Mary that her mother and Mary's mother had been friends. But, when Edith found out about the relationship, Mary was no longer allowed to associate with Arlene. It was that way with anyone who had known Mary's mother.

One day, after making up a story about going to the library to find books for a project, Mary walked to the Schroeder home.

She arrived at the front of a well-kept bungalow, just a few blocks from her home. She looked around and then, satisfied that no one was watching her, she stepped onto the porch and knocked.

Arlene answered the door. "Come on in, Mary. My mother is in the kitchen."

She entered directly into the living room. It was a cozy room with a fireplace and built-in bookcases and there was a broad opening into the dining room. The ceilings, which were slightly higher than her own home, featured redwood beams and the whole atmosphere was warm and inviting.

The girls walked back to the kitchen together. Mrs. Schroeder, a pleasant woman in her mid-forties, looked up from her chores. "Mama, this is my friend, Mary, from school."

"Hello, Mary."

"Nice to meet you, Mrs. Schroeder. Thank you for seeing me. Arlene tells me that you knew my mother, Gwen. Is that so?"

Mrs. Schroeder wiped her hands on the dish towel. "Well, yes, Mary. But, I hesitate to speak with you about her, because I wouldn't want to have Mrs. Beeler mad at me. I still have to live here, you know."

Mary pleaded, "Please, Mrs. Schroeder, please tell me about my mother. I promise that I'll never say you told me anything."

Mrs. Schroeder came out from behind the counter. "Well, alright, Mary. Please, have a seat." She took a breath. "Although I didn't know your mother well, we would visit from time to time."

Mary listened intently.

Mrs. Schroeder continued "She was just lovely and so very nice. She was always so stylish and," she smiled, "I know where you got your beautiful red hair."

Mary blushed, then remained transfixed by Mrs. Schroeder's words as she continued. "Did you know that your father was a high-ranking officer in the Navy?"

"No, I didn't know that." She was so excited that she felt her heart racing in her chest, and she shifted in her seat.

Mrs. Schroeder put a plate of cookies on the table and motioned for Mary and Arlene to help themselves, but Mary took out her school notebook and pencil and prepared to make notes.

"Yes, and I believe his last name was Evans or Ellis. Yes, Ellis, that was the name."

Mary said, "Then, my real last name, before I was adopted, was Ellis."

Mrs. Schroeder nodded her head, "Anyway, when the story came out, my husband was an enlisted man in the Navy, and he said that he knew who the officer was."

Mary sat straight, "What story?"

Mrs. Schroeder delivered lemonade to the girls at the table. "Quite a scandal really. Tongues were wagging. That's for sure."

Mary, anxious for any information, asked "Do you know what it was all about?"

Mrs. Schroeder shook her head. "That's really all I can tell you." She paused a moment, "Oh, yes, there is one more thing I remember. When you were young, you were a rather sickly child, and your mother used to visit the goatherder to get goats' milk for you."

"Oh, thank you so much, Mrs. Schroeder. You don't know what this means to me." Mary closed the notebook and reached for a cookie.

It had been wonderful to be able to speak about her mother with one who had known her. She was filled with hope that she might find the answers to what happened to her family. Her father was an officer in the Navy. That would be a start. That evening at home, even Mother Beeler didn't seem so grim to her.

Mary knew that Kline's Goat Farm, on Saratoga near Sunset

Cliffs, was not far from the Beeler's home. She told Mother Beeler that she was going the library to study and set out for a visit to the goatherder. But, when she got there, Mr. Kline said that he didn't remember her mother and that she must have visited the goat farm which was next to the horse farm, closer to Narragansett Avenue. So, she thanked him and hurried along as it would take longer than anticipated. She didn't want to have to make up excuses for why she was late to Mother Beeler.

When she reached the area, Mary climbed the hill to the cottage and knocked on the door. The goatherder answered. She wiped her hands on her apron, "Yes, what do you want?" She was a woman in her fifties, but she was weathered looking from her days of working out of doors. Her clothes were plain and drab.

Mary was nervous, and answered, "I am told that you knew my mother."

Hands on her hips, "And who was your mother?"

Her name was Gwen and she had red hair. I believe that she used to come to you for goats' milk to give me when I was younger."

There appeared a spark of recognition in her eyes, and she brightened, "Oh, yes, I remember your mother. She was absolutely the most beautiful woman I had ever seen. She was lovely and everything about her was so special. It's been several years since I've seen her. How is she?"

Mary spoke, "She died when I was a little girl, and I was adopted."

"Oh, I am sorry to hear that. She was a real nice woman. I remember her like it was yesterday. Her clothes were so elegant, and I didn't dare compliment her on anything because she would offer it to me. She was very generous. Of course, I wouldn't take anything from her. But then, she fell on hard times, and when she didn't have the money to pay for the milk for you, she would ask me if I would accept her possessions as payment." She raised her hand, "Just one moment. I have something to show you." She turned and entered the cottage.

The goatherder returned, carrying a pocketbook and a fur piece. "You see this alligator purse? She held up the purse for Mary to see. "This was your mother's." Then she showed her the fur piece. "And this was your mother's, too."

Mary reached out to touch them, but the goatherder hugged them closer. Mary regarded the possessions with awe. Then she remembered a white furry wrap that was her mother's. She thought it must have been angora because, when she was little, she would pull the fuzzy hair and rub it between her two fingers and suck her thumb and rub the fuzzies on her nose. The memory made her smile.

The goatherder sighed, "She was so beautiful. Who could ever forget her."

"Do you know where the other children live? There was a boy, Edward, who would be a couple of years older than I, and a girl, Rose, who might be about twelve years old."

The goatherder spoke matter-of-fact. "That was some time ago. I'm afraid that I can't help you. "Well, I must get back to work." She started to turn, then stopped. "But, I do hope you find your family, dear." Then she went back inside.

After a moment of contemplation, Mary turned to leave. She had been thrilled to be so close to personal possessions that had once belonged to her mother. She was filled with hope at finding a remnant of her former life. Who else might have known her mother? She would keep searching.

Chapter 14

1930—The Pennington Connection

I t was just a little over one mile for Mary to walk to Point Loma High School, but it was mostly an uphill climb. The school was opened in 1925 with three hundred eighty students from seventh to twelfth grades, and thirty teachers, staff and faculty. The original building was three stories and of Spanish Mission style exterior with archways at the front entrance, and large multi-paned windows.

The light through the windows cast a soft glow on the cream-colored walls, and Mary found the new school to be warm and inviting. She was a bit anxious about moving up to high school, but then, she had heard from friends that the principal, Mr. Pete Ross, was a wonderful man and that all the students loved him. So, that helped to ease her mind.

Mary and her friend Pat Pennington were talking in the school yard during class break. There were tables and benches provided for the students, and that day the girls shared their lunch and drinks. They had met over the summer at the beach. Pat was beautiful and blonde. She came from wealth and her clothes were the latest in fashion and most expensive. Although Mary's clothes were well made and from current patterns, Pat's clothes were from the top fashion houses; a subtle but noticeable difference in the couture style and fit of the garments. But, Mary was never envious and was pleased to call Pat a friend.

"Pat, how come you're in public school this year? I thought you went to Catholic School."

Pat smiled, "I did. I was at Our Lady of Peace. Only it wasn't so peaceful while I was there."

Mary asked, "Why? What happened?"

Pat made a fake grin, "Like a dummy, I got caught smoking in the cloak room, and they kicked me out. My mother was none too pleased. So, now I'm in purgatory suffering for my sins."

Mary chuckled, "Thank God, I have a partner in crime!"

Pat laughed, and gathered up her books for the next class, then looked up. "Say, Mary, what are you doing this Friday night? We're having a party at my house in Mission Hills."

Mary thought how she would love to go to Pat's party. She had heard that they were fabulous times, but she knew that there was not a chance that she would be allowed to go.

Mary winced, "I'd love to come, but Mother Beeler would never let me go to any party."

Pat spoke pointedly, "Really! Well, just leave that up to my mother, Maisie."

On Friday night, Mary and Mother Beeler waited on the front porch.

Maisie Pennington had spoken with Edith Beeler and told her that there was to be a hot chocolate party, and could Mary come. She said that she would send the chauffeur around to pick her up. Mary saw that Mother Beeler was very impressed. Edith knew that the homes in Mission Hills were grand, and the thought of Mary being introduced to high society pleased her. She would have something to brag about, hobnobbing with the wealthy, and she could drop a name or two, and perhaps raise her standing with the ladies in The Women's Club.

The chauffeur driven limousine arrived, and the chauffeur

came around and held the door open for Mary. She turned and waved goodbye to Mother Beeler who waved back.

Mission Hills was an affluent neighborhood of San Diego located just south of the San Diego River Valley and north of downtown San Diego, overlooking the San Diego Bay. The residents were a colorful mix of families – some old money and others 'nouveau riche'.

The Pennington residence was an imposing Spanish style home on Acadia Drive. There were scenic canyon overlooks and ocean vistas throughout. The entrance floor was terra cotta tile and there were decorative tiles surrounding each archway throughout the first floor. The floors in the main rooms were wide dark oak planks that were highly polished. One of the more casual rooms had redwood beams in the ceiling. The furniture throughout was Mediterranean style, with rich tapestries and cut velvets covering the chairs. As Mary walked through the great room, she admired the furnishings and made note of things she would like to emulate when she had a home of her own.

Maisie, dressed in her finery, a slim flapper style gown of silver lame adorned with several lengthy strands of multi-colored pearls, stood at the door greeting friends. She carried a long cigarette holder with which she gestured her welcome as guests arrived. She was a glamorous dark beauty, part Navajo Indian. Mary thought that she was so stylish compared to Mother Beeler, who seemed frumpy by comparison. She thought of how her own mother was glamorous, as well, and she was happier than she had been in a long time just being there.

A wild party was in full swing. Although it was Prohibition times, everyone held a glass of alcohol. Some couples danced, and lovers slipped off into other rooms. Maisie herself had a taste for the young boys who visited Pat.

Mary sat at the piano playing for the guests who gathered around the piano to sing. Men had come around to have a look at Mary who was unaware of her allure. She was dressed in some of Pat's party clothes and wore makeup. Makeup was never allowed at Mary's home. Pat had large closets and dressing rooms filled with glamorous clothes which she was pleased to share with Mary.

The guests all wanted to sing the popular songs of the day and Mary knew them all. No one had wanted to let her stop playing. But finally, she needed a break for the powder room and promised that she would be right back.

In Pat's room, Mary lounged across the bed, and spoke facetiously, "Some hot chocolate party! This is so great! I never get to do anything fun. Mother Beeler is such a mean old witch. She would just die if she knew the truth." She spoke in sing-song, and thumbed her nose as if to Mother Beeler, "Na, na, na, na, na, na!"

Pat laughed.

Mary continued, "And thanks so much for letting me wear your beautiful clothes – and your glamour make-up!"

Pat asked, "Why doesn't your mother let you do anything?"

Mary spoke in earnest, "She's not really my mother. She adopted me. My real mother died when I was a little girl."

"Oh, that's so sad."

"Mother Beeler never likes anyone I like. I remember when I was in first grade, there was a little girl named Edna Flutter, and her mother was British. Edna said that she was having a birthday party, and I was so excited to be invited. I just loved her, and she was so nice, and her mother was so beautiful. But, Mother

Beeler didn't approve of her, and said that I was not allowed to go to the party. But, I went anyway."

"All of a sudden, into the middle of the party comes the ogre, Mother Beeler, who grabs me by the hair, and yanks me out of the room in front of everyone. I was so humiliated. Everything in my life was a 'no-no'."

Pat shook her head, "Wow, that's terrible! She really is a mean old witch!" She was thoughtful for a moment. "Do you re-member anything about your real family? And what happened to your father?"

"I don't really know. I was told that he was an officer in the Navy. But, I do know that I had a brother and sister. And I don't know what happened to them."

Pat said, "My parents are divorced, but my father was an of-ficer in the Navy, also."

"Do you think I could talk to your mother when she's not busy? Maybe I could ask her advice about locating lost relatives."

Pat threw up her hands, "Why not? She still has a lot of con-nections and Maisie always seems to find a way to get things done."

Mary asked, "Why do you call your mother Maisie?"

"She says it makes her feel old when I call her Mother."

She grabbed Mary's hand and pulled her off the bed. "Let's go back to the party."

The next day after the party, Mary had spoken to Maisie about her family, and Maisie had listened and assured her that she would look into the matter and get back to her.

A few weeks had passed before Pat said that her mother would like to speak to Mary after school that day.

Mary waited anxiously in front of school. Maisie's limo

drove up and the chauffeur came around and opened the door for Mary to get in.

She turned to Maisie. "Hello, Mrs. Pennington."

"Nice to see you again, Mary." She took a drag on her cigarette holder, exhaled, then turned to Mary. "I was able to speak to my friend who is a Naval officer. He told me that he remembered hearing about a Commander Ellis who retired from the Navy and moved to Europe."

Mary brightened, "Do you know where?"

Maisie shook her head, then flicked her cigarette out the window.

"Did you hear anything about my brother and sister?"

"When your mother passed away, her other two children were, most likely, adopted. And in that case, they would have entirely different last names, making locating them highly unlikely."

And with those words, Mary felt her hopes dashed. She tried to swallow, but her throat was dry.

Maisie took another drag on her cigarette holder. She exhaled slowly, then turned to Mary. "So, I'm afraid, Mary dear, that's really all I can tell you."

Mary tried to speak but she was choking back tears. Maisie noticed.

Finally, she managed to say, "But how will I ever find them?"

Maisie answered her matter-of-fact. "Really, Mary, life is too short to spend it in the dreary pursuit of the past. Let it go. You'll be much happier if you do."

Maisie reached over and tapped the chauffeur indicating that she was ready to leave. He came around and opened the door for Mary.

Mary could barely speak she was so let down and her voice quavered. "Well, thank you for trying to help me. I really appreciate it."

Maisie nodded, and Mary stepped out of the car. The chauffeur returned to his seat and the car drove away.

Mary was standing in front of the school feeling forlorn when her boyfriend, Brendan, drove up. They had been friends since elementary school and she had always had a big crush on him. All through junior high Brendan had barely noticed her, but lately they had been keeping company. He rolled down the window and leaned over to speak.

"Hey, Mary. Are you okay?"

Mary looked up, "Not really."

He asked, "How about a ride home?"

"Yeah, thanks."

Mary got in the car and Brendan leaned over and patted her on the knee and grinned provocatively. "We can take a little detour first out to the dunes. A little kiss to make it better. How about it?"

Mary sighed, "Sure, what the heck? Let's go." They drove away.

Chapter 15
1931—School Years

During her Junior year at Point Loma High School, Mary was pulled out of class so many times to play musical accompaniment for other students that she had no chance to fully grasp the concept of algebra. She had been told that musicians were usually good at math, but she thought that she must be the exception.

During the final exam, she was lost. She thought about the consequences she would suffer at home if she failed the exam. As she looked around the room, she could see that Pat was looking in her open book for the answers. Just then, she saw the teacher, Miss Otterbein walking down the aisle towards Pat's desk. She would never forget Miss Otterbein. She had long feet and wore long pointed toe shoes. Mary thought that she should try to warn Pat, but there was no time. Miss Otterbein stopped in front of Pat's desk. "Pat, you can go to the office."

Mary knew that Pat didn't have much to worry about by way of repercussions at home. But Mary was more afraid of Mother Beeler than she was of Miss Otterbein if she received a failing grade. She had been on the honor roll many times and had attended school every day whether she was sick or not.

After class, she saw Miss Virginia Williams, the girl's advisor. Mary told her that she was quite possibly going to fail algebra. And Miss Williams said, "Well, maybe Mr. Ross can do something."

Mr. Pete Ross was the principal who was beloved by everyone at school, students and faculty alike. Mr. Ross thought that

Mary was a wonderful young lady and very talented. He would cut out the articles that were written about her in the newspapers and send them to her with a note of congratulations.

When she came into his office, she cried and told him that she was sure that she would receive a failing grade, and that her life at home would be over.

After a moment's contemplation, he said, "Well, I think we can do something about that. If needed, you can repeat algebra this summer. I will, however, send a note home to Mrs. Beeler. It will explain that you were called upon so many times to lend your musical talents to assist in the school productions, that it made it difficult to you to spend the proper time in your algebra class."

Naturally, Mother Beeler was none too pleased with her failing grade, but she could live with that – the note had softened the blow and she was spared a beating. That summer, Mary and Pat repeated algebra together.

In July of that next year, Mary turned sixteen. She had finished high school and entered San Diego State College on a music scholarship. She was there in her freshman year, 1933, at the same time as Art Linkletter, who was a senior and whom she referred to as a 'big man on campus' type, and her classmate Eldred Gregory Peck, who she thought was a nice guy.

Her friend Pat never made it to college. She ran away and married a man who turned out to be one of those phony evangelical ministers who had learned that Pat came from a lot of money. Later, Mary heard that Pat had, herself, become a minister, and was wearing white robes with purple satin trim, and that she had 'found God'. But, as it turned out, the man that she married was also married to a woman in Mexico who, when she found out that he had married beautiful Pat, reported him to the authorities. So, the ministry was disbanded, and her husband was put in jail for bigamy.

That first year of college, Mary was invited to join the Kappa Theta sorority. She knew the girls were a group of intellectuals, but she would say to her friends that she could never figure out why they wanted her. Having been chastised for so many years, it was difficult for her to recognize just how special she was.

After that she could tell Mother Beeler that she was going to attend her sorority meeting. There were times that she would stay for the first half of the meeting, then excuse herself and duck out the back door to meet her date. She had boyfriends, but everything had to be hidden from home.

In college, she joined the Southern California Glee Club. The group travelled to different states singing and winning awards. She loved the freedom it gave her.

She was a member of the Southwestern Girls Rowing Club which met every Sunday morning at the Southwestern Yacht Club at the foot of Grape Street. She had attended a dance that had been given by the yacht club to promote interest in rowing among young women.

Mary always loved being on the water. She found the repetitive action of rowing to be therapeutic, and she would often let her mind roll on to thoughts of her lost family. She wondered if her mother had enjoyed water sports, and what her brother and sister found interesting in their young lives, and where in this world might they be living. And if she would ever find them.

Chapter 16
1913—The Lovers

Mark entered the dining room of the Palace Hotel and walked to where Gwen was seated. He leaned over to her. "The room number is two-thirty-eight. I will look forward to a knock on my door in about ten minutes."

She reached out and placed her hand on his sleeve. "I have been over this a thousand times in my mind." She looked at him anxiously. "I hope you can understand my hesitancy."

Mark took her hand and kissed it, looked up and smiled warmly, "I understand. And do know that I will love you no matter your decision." He turned and left the room.

Gwen sipped her tea deliberating her decision. She thought that she should just get up and go home. Leave a note of apology for Mark saying that she had thought better of it. That she couldn't act on her feelings, even though she had fallen in love with him. She could think rationally, now that he wasn't in front of her. She knew from the depth of her feelings for him that she was playing with fire. But then, she thought, that wasn't very nice, given that he had told her that he loved her. Didn't he at least deserve an explanation of her misgivings in person?

In room two-thirty-eight, Mark took off his jacket and hung it in the closet. He adjusted the drapes for privacy. He walked to a comfortable chair and sat down, spread his arms on the arms of the chair, crossed his legs and waited.

After a moment or two, there was a knock at the door. Mark

rose and opened the door. The housemaid stood there and hand-ed him fresh linens. "Please let me know if there is anything else you need, Sir."

Mark took the linens. "Thank you. That will be all for now." He shut the door, placed the linens on the bench at the end of the bed, then returned to his chair.

A few moments later, there was another knock. He answered the door. This time it was Gwen. Mark took her hand and led her into the room, closing the door behind her.

"Mark, I came to tell you that I don't think that...."

He took her in his arms and kissed her passionately. "I love you."

She began to speak. "But..."

It was all useless. He covered her lips with his fingers, then kissed her again. She melted in his embrace, and all reserve slipped away.

He slipped off her jacket and dropped it to the floor and be-gan to unbutton her blouse. He kissed her neck.

She reached up and removed her hat. He took out her hair combs, and her hair fell loose around her shoulders. He led her to the bed. He unbuttoned her bodice and she opened his shirt and pulled it down over his shoulders. He took her into his arms and devoured her with his kisses.

They made love, and their rapture was the culmination of all they felt for each other. She was so overcome with emotion that she could hardly breathe. In all her life she had never felt such passion. It was as if he were the enabler who guided her to the heights of ecstasy, and she was swept along in the tide of her emotions.

Later in the afternoon, Mark and Gwen lay in bed under the covers. He was propped up on the pillow; she had her head in the crook of his arm, and her arm draped over him.

Mark stared ahead as he caressed her shoulder. "Have you ever been to Big Sur?"

Gwen answered quietly, "I know of it, but, I haven't been there."

He paused in thought. "I remember the feeling that I had while walking through the area. It was one of sublime completion... that I might like to stay there forever." He turned to Gwen. "And that is how I am feeling at this moment." He leaned over and kissed her.

Then Gwen spoke. "And if I, too, could stay here forever... how perfect."

Mark said, "It might take some time, but it is my intention that we each get a divorce and that we be married."

Any little gnawing doubt she had dissipated with his words of assurance. She wanted to believe him, and so she did. Ever after she would live in a new reality.

He brushed the hair from her forehead. "Now that I have found you, I do not want to do without you in my life."

Gwen whispered, "I will miss you every moment we are apart. You are my everything, my love."

He kissed her, and she melted into his embrace once again.

Guinevere Zepherina Davies

Commander Mark St. Clair Ellis

Chapter 17
1913—San Francisco: A New Life

It was a lovely summer day and Gwen walked around the drawing room at home and stopped to stare out the window. She was lost in thoughts of her lover, Mark. The last few months with Mark in her life had seemed to pass so quickly.

It had been some time since Henry had approached her with affection. He walked up behind her and tried to take her in his arms to kiss her. She backed away, and in that moment, she knew her life there was over. She had crossed the line and there would be no going back to life with Henry.

She took a breath, and then she spoke, "Henry, I want a divorce."

She was relieved that she had told him that she needed to be free. Naturally he was distraught. That next week, she had found a place in San Francisco.

In her room at home, Gwen packed up her belongings and those of Hansie.

Henry entered the room and sat in a chair. He looked ashen. "I don't understand, Gwen. Why are you leaving? What have I done?"

Gwen stopped packing. "It isn't really anything you've done. It's just that we are two very different people, and I just need to be on my own."

Henry implored, "But, I don't understand. Haven't I given you everything to make you comfortable? Haven't I provided for you and Hansie? You know I have always put you first."

Gwen sighed, "I'm sorry, Henry. I just can't live here anymore."

It wasn't that she didn't care about Henry, it was just that she knew that she could no longer exist in this home. She had thought about leaving for some time, but she could never quite find the words nor the right time to speak them. But now circumstances had changed.

She resumed packing and reached for her art supplies.

Henry spoke beseechingly," But, where will you go? How will you get along?"

She continued to pack. "I've taken an apartment in San Francisco. I have some money saved to tide me over. I'll have to find a job, and someone to care for Hansie."

She took a deep breath and stopped packing again. "The truth is, Henry, that I have met someone else."

Shocked, Henry stood abruptly. "Who is this man?"

Gwen paused before forging ahead and then continued. "His name is Mark Ellis. He's an officer in the Navy."

Henry waved his arm in frustration and anger. "What a despicable man to take up with another man's wife!"

He stopped and faced Gwen, incredulous. "And you, Gwen... How could you do this?"

Gwen tried to explain. "Please try to understand, Henry. I was not particularly happy, and it just happened. You and I have not been together in months. Didn't that tell you something?"

She stood in place deliberating her next words. She realized how terrible this would be for Henry. "I am pregnant with his child."

Henry, speechless and defeated, collapsed in the chair.

Gwen came to Henry and knelt before him. She felt so badly about having to hurt Henry when, after all, it wasn't his fault alone. She had married him for a lot of good solid reasons, but she realized that she had never really been in love with Henry, and that the marriage had been a mistake. It simply had not been enough for her.

She told him that she would always care about him and that she hoped in time that he would find the right woman with whom to share his life. When Henry began to cry, Gwen put her head in his lap and cried with him.

Gwen had found a first-floor apartment and Mark had given her the funds to buy the furnishings. She was aware that this was a stretch for Mark's finances, and she did her best to make an attractive and comfortable home while being frugal. She had a great flair for decorating, but she searched out bargains where she shopped. When she was able, she sewed curtains and slip-covers in colorful fabrics and the result was pleasing to the eye.

Henry had requested to have a conference with Mark. Gwen was seated on the front porch with Hansie when he arrived. He walked over to kiss Hansie. and then turned. "Hello, Gwen."

"Hello, Henry. Mark is expecting you." Henry bristled visibly, then turned and entered the home.

In the drawing room, Henry and Mark were in conversation.

Henry spoke stiffly. "What are your intentions regarding my wife, Sir?"

Mark replied, "I plan to do right by her, but unfortunately, my wife is quite ill and I'm afraid the shock of a divorce would kill her. I just can't bring myself to tell her of the present circumstances."

Henry spoke curtly, "Perhaps you should have thought of that before you betrayed her."

Mark ignored the sting. "However, when I am free, it is my intention to marry Gwen."

Henry was thoughtful for a moment. "This is not what I want. But, I love Gwen and I feel that I cannot leave her in these impossible circumstances. So, I will agree to the divorce."

He pointed his finger at Mark. "But, since it is you who is the interloper and who has caused this separation between me and my wife, I will expect you to pay for the divorce. I would also expect you to pay for the expenses incurred with the birth of the child."

Mark responded, "I do agree to pay for both. And I thank you, Sir, for your discretion."

Henry flared up in anger and raised his fist in the air, "By no means do I agree to do this for your benefit!"

Gwen, who had been listening, entered the room. "I know this is difficult for you, Henry. It is a difficult situation for us all. I appreciate your being so fair minded."

When Henry spoke, his voice cracked. "I hope you know what you are doing. Goodbye, Gwen." He turned and walked away.

Gwen felt uneasy and she wasn't sure why. She did know that she had felt completely in control of her home life situation when she lived with Henry, but now this was no longer that same secure feeling. She felt vaguely vulnerable and somewhat anxious. She thought to dismiss the feeling as the 'ups and downs' of pregnancy.

During the next several months, Gwen was at home in the San Francisco apartment that she shared with Mark. At first, she was relieved to be free, but as the months rolled on and she was forced to be somewhat secretive about her living situation, she suffered bouts of loneliness and self-doubt. It would be impossible to have real friendships with other women under the circumstances, and where she was used to holding her head up proudly, now she was always looking over her shoulder for someone to recognize her from her life with Henry. Her sister would come to see her and managed to refrain from offering recriminations. Gwen was five months pregnant with their child, and most of that time, Mark was at sea.

August 19, 1913, Mark was ordered to take the USS Maryland on the Alaskan Coal Investigation Expedition. The United States had purchased Alaska in March 1867, and had begun coal mining in the region. When he arrived at Chilkat, he found that there were seven hundred tons of coal that had previously been mined and deposited on the river bank at Stillwater, during the winter. It was discovered that the equipment furnished the expedition was unsuitable for the purpose of transporting the coal up the swift current of the Bering River. While on location, Mark designed and built twenty-one shallow riverboats. He commented in his report that, 'As a young boy I had experience in building boats for work on a shallow river, and this served me in good stead here.'

Gwen sat reading Mark's letter:

...Our young and tender 'bluejackets' seemed to stand the cold and exposure better than the river men, they acted like schoolboys on a lark. Upon them fell the burden of the work and their enthusiasm and desire to make good carried the day.

Enthusiasm ran high, boats were passing and hallooing at all hours, day and night; competition was on between Indian, sailor, and river men. Enthusiasm, competition, rivalry will get things done, no matter what the hardship.

My own sleeping quarters are in a shack a little removed from the beach, but on stilts over a tidal slough. I could not sleep in the other quarters in the long daylight of Alaskan summer, and the interminable squawking of the gulls. But, as the high tide came up to the floor of my room and a lap of a wave might have reached my cot, I spent many anxious moments wondering whether-or-not the cold waters would, actually, touch my spine where I lay.

The magpies also were a great nuisance. They had the habit of visiting my shack at four a.m. and holding discussions. One morning I got up and shot a magpie and threw his remains on the roof. A few minutes later I heard some 'blue jackets' arguing in a loud tone. I said to them 'Didn't you hear me shoot a magpie a few minutes ago?' They saw the joke and took the hint – the magpies did also, and I was not bothered from either source again.

You are in my thoughts always.

Love, etc.
Mark

Edward Mark Ellis was born December 5, 1913, and Mary Jane Ellis was born July 2, 1916. Both children had red hair and freckles, a sign of their Irish heritage. Gwen adored the children, and Mark said that he always had a soft spot for redheads.

For most of their years together, Mark was at sea. Gwen lived for the times he would come home to her. She knew that homelife with his wife took precedence. She would have to live with that fact. It seemed that she was always waiting. Then, finally, there would be her time. But, she still thrilled to his charms, and his kisses still made her melt.

Mark was made Commander November 26, 1915.

Gwen did not file for final divorce from Henry Dierks until June 30, 1915. Somehow it was her lifeline…just in case. But, at some point, she knew that she needed to let it go.

Final divorce decree granted between Guinevere Dierks and Henry Dierks, February 14, 1917. Custody of minor children awarded Gwen plus thirty dollars per month.

Chapter 18
1934—Ocean Beach

In her room, Mary, now eighteen, sat in a chair sewing up the runs in her silk stockings. She shook her head in exasperation after holding them up and discovering yet two more runs. She thought about the mantra that had become a staple in the face of the Depression, and she repeated it in sing-song, "Use it up, wear it out, make it do, or go without."

Times were very bad. In '29, stockbrokers had been jumping out of the windows. The Depression years that followed were hard on all families. The Beelers had a few rental homes, but those tenants couldn't pay their rent. Fortunately, the Beeler's mortgages were paid off, but there were some friends and neighbors who had lost their homes. Still, there were the expenses of the maintenance and needed repairs on their properties.

Edith was very frugal, and she managed to replace and repair whatever was needed in the rental properties, whenever possible, before she called on the workmen. But, the stress of having to shoulder all the family responsibilities alone made her a bit more testy than usual. She mostly took it out on Gilbert, barking orders at him and reminding him that he was useless to help her.

Although Mary was expected to pitch in, and she did help whenever possible, her school and work made her free time more limited. She hoped to find a job that would allow her the possibility of leaving the Beelers and living on her own. She felt that she had depleted all her sources for information about her family in the town of Ocean Beach. Even so, she felt a responsibility to the family to help in these difficult times, and a job was an absolute necessity in order to pay for college.

San Diego County met the challenge of the Great Depression better than most parts of the Country. There was enough money to build a municipal golf course and tennis courts, to improve the water system, and to open a new Spanish-style campus for San Diego State College. Although Mary did not have the time nor money to play golf, she did learn to play tennis and the availability of the State College made higher education more attainable for many of the young residents of the area.

By the time Mary got to college, there really were no family funds available. She wasn't alone though; in those days all her friends lived on thirty-five cents a day. The Beelers had two cars and Mary drove the old Ford back and forth to San Diego State. Her college friends were happy to chip in for gas and share the ride.

The California Pacific International Exposition, a World's Fair, came to town in 1935. Mary was one of four young ladies from the community chosen to take part in the opening ceremonies. Edith made sure that Mary's gown was perfect for the occasion; long and flowing silk organza with floral trim around the bodice and over the shoulders. The ladies in waiting, as they were called, were to walk down the aisle and step up onto the stage where a large key would be presented which, in ceremony, would officially open the gates to the Exposition. Taking part in the ceremony were town notables, as well as, Governor Frank Merriam, Exposition president, Frank Belcher, and the Ambassador to Mexico, Josephus Daniels.

Over the next two years, there were seven million, two

hundred thousand visitors to the Fair, as well as four hundred exhibits from twenty-three nations. The Exposition left a lasting legacy in the form of Balboa Park which was built in the Mission Revival style. It was located about a mile outside of downtown San Diego, and the animals on exhibit were those that became the start of the San Diego Zoo.

The Exposition boasted a midway with twenty-four-hundred feet of frontage that would present the best shows in existence, to include: 'The Crime Does Not Pay Show,' 'The Two-Headed Baby,' and 'The Snake Farm.' In those days, the midways thrived by presenting the 'freak shows.'

There was to be a 'Midget Village' and they advertised that there were to be over one-hundred 'Lilliputians' that would be living and working there; other advertisements said that some of the midgets were as short as eighteen inches and many weighed less than twenty pounds.

Mary got a job selling orange juice at a stand across from The Midget Village, but there was no refrigeration and customers would complain that they wanted their money back because the juice was sour.

Next door there was a 'girlie show,' and all the motorcycle riders would hang around.

She went there early one morning to set up, and there was one of the midgets waiting for her. He held out his hand and said, "Here, I just got paid, and it's all yours."

After a moment's confusion, she said, "Oh, my God." She was so upset as she realized he must have thought that she was just like the 'girlies' in the show next door. She turned quickly and left the booth.

Since she did not feel comfortable staying in that location, she told the people who ran the orange juice stand about their re-frigeration problem and that she couldn't work there any longer.

She found another job at the Fair at a recording studio, playing piano accompaniment for guests who wanted to sing and make a recording. That job was a breeze for her, but her girlfriends told her about a great job possibility with the Standard Brands Company.

There was a large Spanish Villa with a Mexican orchestra. The girls who worked there would entertain and sing, and would also act as waitresses, serving Chase and Sanborn Coffee, Canterbury Tea, and Royal gelatin puddings. She got the job to play the piano for them. And when she served tea and coffee she received tips. She gave her family her salary, but she kept the tips for herself so that she might have money to leave home.

The manager complimented her on her talent and spoke to her about a permanent job with the company that would involve opening the new locations around the United States. He suggested she would need a business education.

The Catholic school was offering a business course in typing and shorthand that only cost a few dollars a month. Typing came to her easily, but once again, she had a difficult time with shorthand because she was left handed and had been made to write with her right hand.

Mary had been hesitant to speak about the job opportunity at home. For now, there was no need to ruffle feathers, but at some point, she would need to accept the offer to travel with the company.

One day, after much deliberation, she dropped her darning and walked into the sunroom where Dad Beeler was in bed. Shifting from the bed to the wheelchair didn't offer much in the way of exercise, and Gilbert seemed to grow more and more frail with the passing years. He looked up from his book as she entered the room. "Dad, I have a job offer to play the piano for The Standard Brands Company, after the Fair closes."

He smiled, "That's wonderful, Mary! Lately, it's been a real stretch financially. You know that anything that you are able to contribute to the household is very much appreciated."

She took a breath, then continued, "I'm to entertain for the openings of their new restaurant locations around the Country. It's a great opportunity for me. Besides, I wouldn't be gone for long and, of course, I'd be able to send more money home."

Dad Beeler's face fell. "Please don't go, Mary. Don't leave me all alone."

Mary, torn and exasperated, continued, "I can't stay here forever. It's not fair to expect me to give up my opportunities. Don't you love me enough to let me go, so that I can make a life for myself?"

Dad Beeler continued to plead his case, "Just promise me that you'll try to get a job here."

Mary said, "I don't want to get a job here."

"But, Mary, haven't I always done my best to protect you? You know that she will not be fit to live with if you leave. She'll take it out on me."

She heaved a sigh; she was torn. Mary had always had a real sense of responsibility for Dad Beeler's happiness. She used to laugh and say that those born under the sun sign Cancer were always riddled with guilt about something and conflicted about being self-serving. And there it was again. She would see about any other possibilities, but she didn't really want to look. She wanted this job.

Balboa Park Opening Ceremony, Mary Jane Beeler second from the left.

The California Pacific International Exposition 1935

Mary Ellis Beeler in concert

Chapter 19
Early 1918—San Francisco

Mark remained married to Elizabeth. In her heart, Gwen could not have ill will towards his wife; still, she looked forward to the day that he was free, and their own relationship could be affirmed.

This day, Mark entered the apartment, then burst in the drawing room, threw down his jacket and hat. Hansie was in his wheelchair. Edward, age five, and Mary Jane, age two, played with Tinker Toys on the floor. They jumped up and ran to Mark. Gwen, who was pregnant with their third child, stopped straightening up the room.

She was always happy to see him arrive, but it meant that she had to try to keep things perfect and that wasn't always easy to do with three young children at home. Mark was fastidious about his person and demanded that his surroundings be in good order, as well. There would be the usual clutter of toys around the room to be tidied up, and crayon paintings on the walls to be scrubbed clean.

Edward and Mary Jane shouted, practically in unison, "Daddy, Daddy, you're home!"

Mary Jane ran to Mark, "Did you bring us a 'prise?"

Mark hugged the children absentmindedly. "No, no, children. Not this time. Now, run along and play in the next room, please. I have some things to discuss with your mother."

The children, disappointed, returned to their play in the next room.

Mark paced back and forth in the room, and Gwen took a seat.

"Elizabeth has found us out. I don't know who said something, but she has been made aware."

Gwen spoke with empathy, but secretly she was glad to be affirmed. "Mark, I'm so sorry. I know how difficult that must be for you."

Oblivious, Mark continued, "Yes. and I'm sure you understand how important it is for me to guard my reputation. If this situation were to become known to my superiors, I would lose my standing in the Navy. I would lose everything I have worked for all these years. Surely you can see how important it is for our future to prevent that from happening. I can't see any other way other than to implore you to leave the San Francisco area, immediately."

She stood and threw up her hands in frustration. "That's ridiculous! We've been together for six years. Don't you think someone was bound to notice?" She paced the room, then faced Mark, hands on her hips, "Why should I have to move? I have every right to be here. I am the mother of your children."

Mark had walked over to the window and closed the curtains. He turned back to Gwen and tried to reason. "When one becomes an officer in the Navy, it is understood that you must conduct yourself as a gentleman. There can be no hint of impropriety in your life. Therefore, under the present circumstances, if it can be proved that we cohabitate, I will be dismissed from the Navy."

Gwen sat once again. She had been waiting for years, secretly hoping that his wife would find out and divorce him. She spoke pointedly. "Well, Mark, if your wife has been told about us, it certainly doesn't appear that the news has killed her. So, why don't you just ask her for a divorce?"

"Don't be ridiculous, Gwen. I am counting on my marital inheritance to support our lives in the future. Contrary to your thoughts, I can't possibly live well on my Navy pay alone and

I can't bear the thought of our association becoming public knowledge. All that tongue wagging and gossiping is just too impossible for me to imagine. I have always prided myself on being respectable."

Her voice raised to a higher pitch, "Oh, but it's all right for me not to be respectable?" She was exasperated by the whole conversation.

His arms held out, he beseeched her. "Please, Gwen."

Her heart sank. "At this point, I have only your word that you will do the honorable thing and marry me."

"Of course, I am going to marry you. How could you possibly think differently? I love you."

Gwen felt utterly vulnerable. This move would be a hardship for her, but it seemed there was no other way. Here she was pregnant and having to pull up stakes and run like a scared rabbit. She wanted to scream and cry, but that wouldn't be attractive. All things considered, she was grateful that they were together, so that was that.

She stood up straight. "All right, Mark, I will make the arrangements to move, but I won't like it!"

Mark walked over to Gwen and put his arms around her. "Try to understand, Gwen, our future is at stake... 'Our' future!"

Gwen's demeanor softened. She sighed in resignation. She loved him, and she believed that he loved her.

Mark continued, "Thank you, dear, for being understanding." His hand under her chin, he turned her face to his. "Sorry about this turn of events. It will be good when we can put all this behind us and spend our lives together." He kissed her, but it was bittersweet for Gwen.

She would keep a hopeful heart. After all, she thought, he was in a very difficult position.

Chapter 20
1936—San Diego Office of the Gas and Electric Co.

A friend had told Mary about a temporary job at the Gas and Electric Company to replace a secretary who was out on maternity leave. So, half-heartedly, she applied for the position. She felt compelled to stay and look after Dad Beeler for a time, and she was told that this would only be a temporary position. It would be a bitter disappointment to give up on her dream job.

At age twenty, and quite pretty with a nice figure, Mary was given dictation by her prospective boss. Ray Brown sat back in his swivel chair, facing the side wall. He was in his mid-fifties and showed a bit of a paunch.

Mary was lost. Ray was dictating at a lightning speed, and Mary tried concentrating, but to no avail. She was fast becoming overwhelmed. Finally, she gave up trying. So, without saying a word, she simply got up, placed the pen and paper on the desk, and started to leave the office.

She thought this was most definitely not where she wanted to be, and certainly not working for Ray Brown, who gave her the creeps. She thought that he leered rather than looked at her, and that was certainly not a comfortable feeling.

Ray spun around in his chair to see her leaving. "Miss Beeler, where are you going?"

Mary turned at the door and faced Ray. "I can write an ordinary letter, but I can't take this dictation which involves all these technical terms about which I know nothing."

"Please sit down, Miss Beeler, and let's try this again."

Mary took the paper and pen and sat down once again. He then proceeded to dictate a letter that Mary thought any 'two-year-old' could have written. He had eliminated all the technical terms and had spoken as slow as a snail.

When she was finished, he said, "Thank you very much, Miss Beeler."

Mary returned the paper and pen and left the office. She was glad to be leaving.

Back home at the Beeler's, Mary walked in the door.

Dad Beeler called from his bed. "Mary, they just called from the Gas and Electric Company to say that you have the job!"

Mary burst into tears.

As it turned out, Mary agreed to work at The Gas and Electric Company because she would be able to finish business school at the same time. She always believed that it was best to be prepared because you never knew where life would take you, and certainly it was a requirement for her prospective dream job. And it was, after all, only a temporary position. But then, circumstances changed at the office and somehow the job became permanent. Mary wrestled with her conscience, but she just couldn't desert Dad Beeler. She felt compelled to pass on the position that included travel, and at that point she knew she was stuck there.

Mary resigned herself to life at the Gas and Electric Company. She worked with about one hundred engineers.

She was seated at her desk, which was surrounded by cubicles housing the various engineers, and concentrated on the paperwork before her. Ted Rockwell, a pleasant looking man, mid-thirties, sat at the neighboring desk drawing a doodle. He walked over to Mary's desk and dropped the paper in front of her.

She looked up at Ted. "Hey! You're a regular Norman Rockwell!

Ted grinned, "I am a Rockwell, and Norman happens to be my cousin." Ted assumed a quizzical posture. "I have no idea why he is more famous than I. They must be blind." Mary laughed. Ted smiled, "Welcome to work at the Gas and Electric Company. Happy to have you here, Mary. We need a pretty face along with all these mugs."

She nodded her head, "Thank you, Ted."

Mary held up the page and viewed it. "I'm going to frame this doodle. Then I can say, I knew him when!"

Ted chuckled. "Don't hold your breath."

Ray Brown leaned out of his office. "Mary, can you come into my office?"

She rolled her eyes, "Be right there."

The girls in the office had warned her about Ray and 'his ways,' and she was on guard. She picked up a pad and pen and walked to his office.

Ray sat at his desk. Mary took a chair opposite him. "I need to send a letter to all department heads regarding some changes in company policy. Why don't you pull your chair over here next to my desk, so that I can review as you write." Mary brought her chair closer. "Closer, Mary - right here next to me."

She brought the chair closer and sat. Ray reached out and patted her on the knee. "There now, Mary. I won't bite. I just appreciate a beautiful girl when I see one." He started to rub her thigh.

Mary jumped up and moved away. "Please don't do that!"

Ray Brown put up both his arms as if to back off. "All right, all right! Just sit down and let me dictate the letter "

She sat once again, and the dictation began. She thought that Ray Brown was a big jerk and she wondered why in the world he thought he could take such liberties with her. But, she knew that she was not the only one he approached. She needed the job, but she would make sure to keep her distance from that lecherous old fool!

When the executives found out about her musical abilities, she was asked to play the piano for the company functions. She joined the G&E Girls Rowing Team, and in general settled into life there at the Gas and Electric Company.

One day, as she read the paper, Mary missed her usual stop and she alighted from the bus in front of 235 Broadway, a six-story white masonry building with columns at the entry. The sign above the door read, The Union Building. Additional signs announced *The Daily Union Newspaper* and *The Evening Tribune*. She looked up at the signs and was thoughtful. She had been told there was a scandal involving her mother and father. And she knew that the last name was Ellis and that her father was an officer in the Navy. Perhaps there was something written in the paper in those years that would be useful.

She was nervous as she walked up to the door and entered the building. She approached the front desk, and spoke to the front desk clerk, a man in his fifties who was totally engrossed in reading a book. "Excuse me, sir, but do you have an archives department?"

The gentleman told her of the hours for the research library, and she thanked him for his time.

Back at the Gas and Electric Company, Mary and Ted were seated at a long table in the employee's lunch room. As they opened their brown bag lunches, Mary said, "On the way to work, I made an interesting discovery. We're only four short blocks from the newspaper offices."

"I did know that, but why the interest in the newspaper?"

"Do you believe in Karma, Ted?"

He looked up. "Sometimes. Why?"

"I'm going to start looking for information about my father on my lunch hour. So, you'll need to find a new 'brown bag' buddy for a time."

"So, you're trading me in for a bunch of old newspaper copy? But, why don't you start looking in the library files? It's cleaner, brighter, and only one block away."

"Good idea." She sipped her drink. "I want to find out what happened to my family but, at the same time, I'm a little afraid of what I might find. I know my father's name, but after all this time, he probably isn't even alive. It's very disheartening and I've been disappointed before. It's as if my happiness hangs on the answers I might find."

Ted was thoughtful for a moment, "They say if we look hard enough, we all have a 'horse thief' or two in our family history. You can't live your life in fear. You're a wonderful girl, Mary, and you're stronger than you might think. Remember, 'the truth will set you free'. Go find your truth."

"Thanks, Ted." Mary knew her friend was right. Nothing ventured, nothing gained as the saying went. It was just that she had had been hopeful for so long, and now she would have to be prepared for the outcome, whatever that might be.

After two weeks of going through files and poring through the records that started with 1916, the year of her birth, Mary was about to give up the newspaper search. Then, just as she was closing the last newspaper for the day, she turned the page and saw a picture and article about Commander Mark St. Clair Ellis. She read on:

In command of the Samoan Expedition in 1915, Ellis took the U.S.S. Neptune safely to Samoa and brought back the U.S.S. Princeton to the United States. The Princeton had been wrecked months before he arrived, and he brought her home safely, although she looked so badly that the pumps were kept running and the men, for thousands of miles were constantly in readiness to abandon ship.

Ellis was commended for heroism on July 9, 1917, upon the occasion of the great explosion at the Naval magazine, Mare Island, California. Although injured by the explosion and bleeding profusely, he took charge and put out a fiercely blazing fire in a dry cotton house, same being only a few feet from high explosive magazine. Had Ellis failed to act heroically and promptly, many more lives and millions of dollars of Government property would unquestionably have been destroyed. For this Ellis was also commended by Admiral Earle.

She continued reading and made notes. Mark was a veteran of both the Spanish American War and World War I. During the Spanish American War, he served as a junior officer in a gunboat and participated in the battle of Santiago Bay. He became an ordnance expert and was the inventor of a Self-Scoring Target System that was used in Naval gunnery for many years. He was promoted to work in the Atlantic for which he was awarded the

Silver Star medal. As she read, Mary felt something that had, to date, been elusive to her: pride.

Back home, Mary walked into the sunroom and spoke pointedly to Dad Beeler. "Why didn't you tell me that my father was a Commander in the Navy?"

Dad Beeler sat upright in bed. "How did you find that out?"

Mary didn't answer. She simply stared at him.

He buckled. "Mary, please promise me that you won't let on that you know anything about this to Mother."

She thought about it and realized that there would be hell to pay if Mother Beeler found out that she knew about her father. After a moment's deliberation Mary sighed, "All right, I won't say anything to her right now. But, I want some answers."

"I can't tell you anything."

She said, "Can't? Or won't?"

Gilbert Beeler became tight lipped. "You should leave well enough alone. No good will come from prying into the past. No good at all!"

She pressed on, "I want the truth."

Completely exhausted with the effort, Gilbert said, "The truth will only hurt you, Mary. I've always hoped to shield you from that; to protect you, and now you want to open yourself up to heartache. Please, I beg of you."

Just then Mother Beeler walked in. "What are you two talking about?"

Gilbert was quick to reply, "Nothing, Mother."

She shot him a skeptical glare. He dismissed Mary and picked up his book and started to read.

She spoke to Ted the next day at work. "I would like to find out where Mark Ellis is buried. I doubt that he is still alive, him being in the war and all."

"With the enormous presence of the Navy right here in our area, why not call the office of The Department of the Navy in San Diego. I'm sure they'll be able to direct your search."

That afternoon, Mary called and spoke with the secretary in the office of records. "But, can't you tell me anything?"

"Any information about Commander Ellis would be in personnel records with the Department of the Navy in Washington, D.C., and someone in the Navy would need to make an official request for that to be given out."

Mary sighed, "I see. Well thank you for your time." Disappointed, she hung up the phone and tried to think of what else she might do to find out any information concerning the whereabouts of Commander Mark Ellis.

THE NEWS-METER

Published in the Interest of its Employees by the San Diego Consolidated Gas & Electric Company

VOLUME XIII, No. 5   MAY, 1937

DOWN TO THE SEA WITHOUT SHIPS

This arresting still is a dry-land view of the Gasco members of the Southwestern Girls Rowing Club. Any Sunday morn you may see them shoving off from the Southwestern Yacht Club in their 8-oar shell for a two-hour workout. Don't be misled by the lack of visible biceps. These girls can churn up the Bay like a Mississippi sidewheeler. They are: Mary Schneider (Commercial), Florine Schutz (Billing), Marge Miller (Purchasing), and Mary Jane Beeler (Record).

May 1937 Gas and Electric Womens' Rowing Team, Mary Jane Beeler
(Top photo center, bottom photo right)

Chapter 21
Hotel del Coronado

That next Spring, on a Friday night, Mary and her college sorority sister, Winnie Kech, took the ferry over to Del Coronado and then hopped the streetcar to the Hotel Del Coronado. The dances at the hotel were the social highlight of the community, and the girls looked forward to each evening with renewed excitement.

The hotel was a spectacular Victorian style building; white, with red roofs throughout.

They entered the hotel and walked through the beautifully decorated lobby. The entire room was embellished with tall carved pillars of dark Illinois oak. The carved ceilings were of intricately carved oak, as well. The floors were carpeted in a lush green with diamond-shaped patterns throughout. Chairs were covered in floral patterns of peonies, and there were numerous tall jardinieres filled with palms. Sheraton-style tables of dark mahogany held tall vases of beautiful flowers, and the whole effect was one of substantial elegance. Through the large archways, there were comfortable outdoor seating areas of rattan furniture with umbrella tables. All were surrounded by magnificent gardens, and the perfume wafted through the halls.

As they continued down the halls, they passed the main dining room and breakfast rooms on the right, which seated hundreds of guests. Then, they turned left down the hall to the grand ballroom with its highly polished hardwood floors. The ballroom was under the main turret and boasted an enormously high domed ceiling. Tall windows surrounded the entire room and additional smaller windows continued through the upper part of the arched sides of the room.

The girls each wore elegant slim satin gowns that shimmered as they walked, Mary in green and Winnie in blue, and heads turned as they entered the ballroom.

On stage, Duke Ellington was dressed in white tails, and the band played *It Don't Mean a Thing, If It Ain't Got That Swing.*

Mary looked around the room. "This is so, so exciting. I just love this music!"

"Yes. Isn't this just the best!"

"Oh no, Winnie. "I think the 'best' is all these gorgeous young Naval officers I see before me."

She had hoped that she might meet the right officer who would be willing to help her find some answers about Mark Ellis.

Winnie laughed, "You're right! Whatever was I thinking! Come on. I see an open table."

As they walked to a table, all eyes followed them. They took a seat and looked around the room. It wasn't long before two young officers approached; both were handsome and in their dress uniforms. When they arrived at the table, one of the officers leaned over to Mary, "Are you girls looking for Harry and Jim?"

Mary shook her head, "No."

"No?" He straightened up, smiling broadly. "Well, then, you must be looking for us!"

The girls laughed and Mary asked, "And who are you?"

"Lieutenant George Roberts, but my friends call me Buzzy. And this is my friend, Lieutenant Robert Cooper, better known as Bob. May we join you?"

In unison, the girls said, "Please do."

The men took a seat at the table. There was the usual chit-chat about 'where are you from' and 'how long have you been here.'

Buzzy asked Mary to dance and Bob and Winnie followed them to the dance floor. After they finished the dance, Buzzy asked Mary if she would join him out on the porch so that he might have a cigarette. They walked out together and as they stood overlooking the ocean, Mary found him charming and easy to talk to. She decided to take a chance and take him into her confidence. "You seem like a guy who knows his way around."

Buzzy smiled, "I get along. Why?"

Mary posed a question, "If someone wanted to get information from Navy records, what do you know about that procedure?"

He tilted his head, "I suppose I could have access. Why? What are you looking for?" Mary told him about herself, and that she had been adopted as a child. She spoke to him about her discovery about her father. She said that she would like to find out about him; that he had been an officer in the Navy, but she had been told that she would need official request to get any information. Then she asked if he thought he might be able to help her, and he smiled and told her that he would certainly see what he could find out for her.

She said, "That would be so swell, and I would be ever so grateful for your help."

"Tell me what you know about your father."

He was so easy to talk to that Mary felt as though she had found a new friend. Buzzy was quite taken with Mary, yet even though he was a handsome man, there was no spark of romance on her part. She just really liked him. They went back into the ballroom and danced the night away. When the girls left for the evening they talked non-stop all the way home about their wonderful stroke of luck to have met two such elegant young Naval officers – handsome and great dancers. And, of course, Mary was thrilled to have made an important connection in her search for information about her father.

On that Sunday, Buzzy stood on the Beeler's porch and knocked on the door. Edith Beeler walked to answer it. When she opened the door, she asked, "May I help you?"

Buzzy bowed slightly, "Yes, Ma'am. I'd like to speak to Mary Beeler. Is she home?"

"No, she's not here. To what is this in reference?"

Buzzy hesitated, "Yes, Ma'am. I'm Lieutenant George Roberts. I was supposed to call Mary at work, so I don't mean to bother you. But, this is Sunday, and I just received word that I am being shipped out first thing in the morning. If it wouldn't be too much trouble, would you give her a message?"

Edith answered, "Certainly. What is your message?"

Buzzy handed her a note. "Please tell her that I have spoken to Lieutenant Parker at the Navy Department in Washington, and he is expecting her call. If you would be so kind as to give her this note. Just tell her that he'll be able to answer her questions regarding her father."

She stiffened, "Thank you. I'll give her the message."

She shut the door. Her face darkened, and she tore up the note.

Chapter 22
1937—The Letter

The next day in the office, Mary sat typing at her desk. Her cheek was bruised and swollen. The previous evening, there had been a big row with Mother Beeler over the visit from Buzzy. Disappointed, she knew there wasn't any point in asking her for any information he might have left; it wouldn't be forthcoming.

Ted walked by and stopped short. "Hey what happened to you?"

Mary spoke through gritted teeth. "Oh, nothing."

Ted grunted, "That's some nothing." He walked on.

She took out a compact mirror. Her hand went to her cheek, then her face became emboldened. Immediately, Mary picked the phone, looked at her note pad, and dialed a number. She would ask that the long-distance call be deducted from her pay. An operator answered on the other end. "United States Department of the Navy. How may I direct your call?"

Mary inquired, "May I please speak to someone in the personnel records department."

"One moment please."

There was a short wait while Mary was transferred. "Office of Records. Lieutenant Andrews speaking."

"Hello, Lieutenant Andrews. This is Mary Jane Beeler, of San Diego, California. A friend in the Navy, Lieutenant George Roberts, suggested I call regarding my search for a relative of mine."

Lieutenant Andrews answered, "I'm not at liberty to give out that information."

Mary was choked with emotion, "Please, Sir. The person I'm trying to locate is my father. His name is Commander Mark St. Clair Ellis. I've been searching desperately for any news of him. Her voice cracked, "Please, please help me. I don't have anywhere else to turn."

There was a pause. Then Lieutenant Andrews asked, "And who did you say referred you to this office?"

Mary answered, "Lieutenant George Roberts is his name, sir."

Ted looked up from his paperwork. Mary stood beside his desk with a paper in hand. "Commander Mark St. Clair Ellis is still very much alive and living in Annapolis, Maryland. And I have his address!"

Ted smiled and threw his papers in the air in celebration. Then he stood up and gave her a big hug. She was so thrilled with her discovery. They spoke about the letter she would write. She said that she was nervous about contacting him.

"I can understand your hesitancy but, of course, you must set aside your fears and write to him."

She knew that was true.

Later that day, when she had a break from office work, she sat to compose a letter to her father whom she had not seen since she was a very young child. She struggled with her words.

June 22, 1937.
Dear Sir,

This is a most unusual letter for a daughter to be writing to her father. Although you have not been a part of my life since I was a small child, I would appreciate knowing about your life, and the reasons that you chose to live apart from our family.

I am now age twenty, and I have lived with the Beelers, my adoptive family, since I was five years old. My brother, Edward, and my sister, Rose, have been lost to me since that time. As well, I have had no idea of your whereabouts, that is, until just recently.

I have been to college and I am a graduate of the Los Angeles Conservatory of Music. I have a good job, so please do know that I have no interest in your money. But, I long to find my brother and sister, and I would most appreciate an explanation for what transpired between you and our mother, Gwen. Our world was forever changed with the ending of your relationship.

For reasons of privacy, please address any correspondence to me at the Gas and Electric Company where I am presently employed.

I await your reply,
Mary Ellis Beeler.

When she finished the letter, she walked over to show it to Ted for his review.

"I think it's an excellent letter, Mary."

So, she placed the letter in an envelope and addressed and stamped it. Then, she put on her jacket and left the office.

She stood in front of the post office and tapped the letter with her fingers in a moment of contemplation. Finally, she took a deep breath and walked inside and dropped it in the mail chute.

Chapter 23
1918—San Jose Cottage

Gwen had moved to an apartment in San Jose at the urging of Mark. She was growing weary of this lifestyle and looked forward to settling in permanently to her life with him. She had read that Mark's wife had died earlier in the spring, and she had written to him to say that she was sorry for his loss.

Dearest One,

I have read of the sad news of the passing of Elizabeth Ellis. I am aware that she had been suffering for some time. Since you were together for several years, this must be a very difficult time for you, and I wish I could be there to console you. Do try to take comfort in knowing that she will now be resting in peace.

Please let me know when you have been able to conclude your personal affairs in your marital home. I long for the time when we are together so that I might give you a hug in person.

The children and I miss you terribly.

I love you,
Gwen

It was the end of May and Gwen and Mark's third child, Rose Ellis, had been born on April 28, 1918 in San Jose. The one-month-old baby lay in her bassinet in the sun room. Mary Jane, age two, played with her dolls on the floor. Hansie, now seven, was in his wheelchair, which he managed to manipulate very well. And while he couldn't speak well, he was intelligent and cheerful and laughing most of the time.

He loved to be taken out to see the city where they lived. Once his wheelchair got away from Gwen and rolled down a long hill and crashed over. With despair, Gwen expected to see him crushed under the chair, but there he was laughing with glee at the exciting ride.

There was a knock at the door. Gwen answered the door and smiled. "How nice to see you again, Matt."

Matt Lovett, a seaman under the command of Mark Ellis, stood with a newspaper tucked under his arm. He was a tall, well-built and handsome man. Matt has been the messenger delivering her household support each month from Mark, and Gwen and Matt had become close friends over the past few years. She had yearned for female friendships but that hadn't been possible under the circumstances. Matt had become her lifeline to the outside world. He was a comfortable person to be around...empathetic to her situation, and a man with a kind heart. Often, he would stay for dinner and Gwen was delighted to have a man to cook for, and the children loved his company.

Matt walked into the room and handed her an envelope containing her household support from Mark. "I am happy to be the messenger, I look forward to these visits."

"Thank you." She took the envelope. "May I offer you a drink of something? Tea or perhaps something stronger?"

"A cup of tea sounds great."

Gwen walked back to the kitchen. Matt followed. "Edward

is in school. But, Mary Jane and my new baby, Rose, are here, and, of course, my sweet Hansie. They will all be delighted to see your smiling face again."

Matt walked into the sun room. Mary Jane looked up and smiled. He walked over to the children and bent down to kiss Mary Jane's head.

Then he walked over to Hansie. "Hello, Hansie, dear fellow. You are looking quite well today." Hansie smiled at Matt in return. He walked over to the bassinet and looked down at the baby. "Gwen, she is really a beautiful baby."

Gwen called from the kitchen, "Thank you. Of course, I think that she's perfectly lovely."

Matt walked back into the kitchen and took a seat at the table. Gwen prepared a pot of tea. She looked his way and smiled. Then her hand went to her back and she grimaced. She had been feeling pain for some time now, but she was afraid to acknowledge that she should seek medical advice. Whatever the findings, she certainly would not have been able to take the time off to rest with no one else to see after the children.

"What's wrong, Gwen?"

"It's my back. It's like a dull ache in the middle of my back. Maybe I'm lifting things the wrong way."

Matt spoke sympathetically, "You should see a doctor."

She was quiet for a moment. She knew that there would not be enough for a doctor's care with what Mark was sending her for support, and she was reticent to ask for more. She hoped to be as little a burden as possible.

She brought the teapot to the table, then paused and reflected. "If I could do it over, I would do it all differently. My mother used to say, 'You can never build your happiness on the unhappiness of others.' And she was right."

She set the cups and saucers on the table. She poured the tea, offered the milk pitcher and sugar pot, but he waved his hand and declined both. She sat and smiled at Matt.

Matt took a sip of his tea. Then he sighed and put down his cup. "Gwen, I have something to show you. And I didn't want you to be alone when you read it."

She was taken back. "Whatever is it?"

Matt unrolled the newspaper. He opened it to the society page and handed it to Gwen. She looked at Matt hesitantly, then she began to read:

Naval Officer Weds Millions. San Francisco Examiner May 19, 1918. Commander Mark St. Clair Ellis takes Mrs. Helen Rood as bride.

Gwen looked up at Matt in disbelief. She looked back at the paper and continued with a shaky voice.

"USN, long stationed at Mare Island, he gained international reputation as an inventor of military devices and was secretly married here yesterday to Mrs. Helen Allen Rood of Seattle. The bride, known as the Silver Mining 'Bonanza Queen,' is one of the wealthiest women of the Northwest. Her former husband, Hugh Rood, went down with the Titanic."

Gwen looked up at Matt as she finished speaking.

"The wedding had been planned for some weeks hence."

Gwen was visibly destroyed. She stood and walked around the room and threw up her arms in utter disbelief. Then she stopped and faced Matt. "He used to tease me and say, 'You wouldn't stand in my way if I had the opportunity to marry a rich woman, once my wife dies.' I'd flare up and he'd pass it off as a joke."

Gwen grabbed her hair as if to tear it out. She cried out loudly in anger. "How could I have been such a fool? How could I be so blind?"

Matt stood and walked over to her. He took her hands in his. "You are not a fool. He's the fool!"

Gwen buried her face in his shoulder and began to sob. "After all this time, I had expected him to marry me for the sake of our children, if for no other reason."

Matt pulled out his handkerchief and handed it to Gwen.

She spoke between muffled sobs "Thank you."

Matt spoke tenderly, "What will you do now, Gwen?"

She tried to pull herself together. "I don't know. I need some time to think... to let this all sink in."

Chapter 24
Helen Allen Webster
Stoiber Rood Ellis

G wen's sister told her that a friend of hers had seen an article written about Mark's new wife. In her own world, it pained Gwen to be the brunt of ridicule and gossip, but there was nothing to do about it. She knew that she had brought it on herself and that was a bitter pill to swallow. Gwen had been so naïve to trust that her situation would right itself, but it had not turned out well. She retrieved a copy of the magazine:

Helen Allen Webster Stoiber Rood Ellis, known as The Bonanza Queen, is one of the greatest of Colorado characters — a woman to rank in legend with Baby Doe Tabor and the Unsinkable Mrs. Brown. She has had two fortunes and four husbands, and she was a leader of Denver Society.

Polly Fry, a famous Denver society reporter at the turn of the century, described her as 'first, last and all-time a manager. She has managed Mr. Stoiber beyond the wildest hope of woman. She bought and managed the Silver Lake Mine, and sold it for $1,000,000 cash, if not more.'

'She came to Denver and managed to scatter the blackballs which a discerning few dropped into the basket at the Woman's Club election. She would step on the train of your gown and not offer you a pin to fasten yourself together.'

'Never let the heart manage the head,' is Mrs. Stoiber's sentiment.

The first we know of Mrs. Stoiber was when she came to Gunnison as a bride with her husband, Hugh Webster, a member of the law firm of Cobb & Webster. A short time later, they moved to Grand Junction. Mrs. Webster was about twenty at the time, and was recalled later as 'a handsome, buxom woman, quite pretty, rather imperious in her manners, with a fiery temper.' Webster was a quiet, unassuming man, completely different in personality from his wife.

After two years in Grand Junction, the Websters moved to Silverton. Webster disappeared from Mrs. Stoiber's life a short time later. Whether he died is not known.

Her next husband was Edward Stoiber, who conducted an assaying and sampling works at Silverton and also had mining interests there. Stoiber was highly educated, a graduate of Freiburg and other technical schools of Germany. With Mrs. Stoiber, he developed the Silver Lake Mine and Mill and sold it to the Guggenheim Exploration Co. for $2,000,000.

When they moved to Denver, the Stoibers found a place in society, unlike the Browns and some of the other mining rich who tried to crash the sacred portals. With the years, Mrs. Stoiber gained weight, lost much of her beauty and is said to have become more imperious than ever.

The Stoibers traveled extensively abroad, gathering art treasures for the home they planned to build one day in Denver. It was on one of these trips, on April 21, 1906, that Stoiber died in Paris of typhoid fever.

Following Mr. Stoiber's death, Mrs. Stoiber entertained many suitors. In 1909, she married Hugh Rood, a highly respected businessman, vice president of Seattle Creosote Company. Rood lost his life in 1912 with the sinking of the Titanic. Mrs. Rood was saved from the disaster only because she had decided to stay an extra week in London and take a later ship. Rumors persisted, cropping up all over the world, that Rood still was alive. Mrs. Stoiber-Rood spent a fortune in the search for him, but never located him.

As his widow, she inherited $2,500,000. She married again in 1918. The bridegroom was Commander Mark St. Clair Ellis, U.S.N.

After reading the article, Gwen decided to seek advice from a lawyer. She would need help in securing a life for herself and the children. Mark should certainly be responsible for the support of his three children. She had been the fool long enough. She would dry her tears and think with her head instead of her heart.

Mark's support had continued for the time being but, she had no assurance that she would receive support in the future. She believed the children deserved that security.

Mark kept sending her letters saying please let me explain, but she had no intention of further association with him and certainly not entanglements with his new wife who sounded formidable.

She was disgusted that Mark should have married such a woman. She could not imagine that he could love someone so cold and calculating. Though, after his behavior of late, she thought that they probably deserved one another. She had been heartbroken, but somehow it felt better to be angry. Gwen had found it particularly galling when she read that the wedding had taken place at the Palace Hotel.

She visited the law offices of Horton L. Titus and Frank J. Macomber. But the moment she filed the paternity court case, and notices were sent out, her child support ceased to arrive. She was left with no way to pay for her lodging, nor food for the family, and no funds for medical expenses. With no savings, it wasn't long before she was destitute.

Chapter 25

1918—Aboard Ship

While under Mark's command on the USS Harford, the artist Norman Rockwell painted the portraits of both Commander Ellis and his wife, Helen Allen Ellis. The portrait of Commander Mark St. Clair Ellis is one of Norman Rockwell's earliest portraits in oil and copy appears in a catalogue of his works titled 'Norman Rockwell, A Definitive Catalogue,' by Moffatt, page 977, Plate 31.

An excerpt from an article published March 5, 1960, Saturday Evening Post, in the words of Norman Rockwell:

A new commander had been appointed to the Charleston Naval Base. A sailor named O'Toole was discussing the situation with me one afternoon when the studio door was flung open, a voice yelled "ten-SHUN!," and in walked the new base commander, a big, handsome, beefy-looking fellow in dress uniform. His smartly dressed wife accompanied him. 'Carry on, men, carry on,' he said. I went back to work on a portrait, and O'Toole fussed with a pile of old canvasses in the corner. The new commander looked at the portrait on my easel, asked about my work and left. O'Toole said that the new commander could be 'got around,' but the wife worried him.'

The next day, I was transferred to the commander's personal staff and went to live on the U.S.S. Hartford, which had been Admiral Farragut's flagship during the Civil War. Now, it was moored in

Charleston Harbor as the official headquarters and residence of the commander of the Charleston Naval Base. The Hartford had been refurbished since its fighting days in Mobile Bay. A grand, red-carpeted staircase swept down to a ballroom decorated with hand-carved scrollwork. The staterooms, which were officers' quarters, were hung with velvet tapestries.

I shared a plush stateroom with a tenor and O'Toole, whom I had placed as chauffeur on the base-commander's staff by drawing a portrait of the ensign in charge of transportation. When the commander entertained visiting dignitaries, the tenor sang, and I displayed my work before the assembled guests.

I soon learned that one of my jobs on the Hartford was to paint portraits of Commander Mark St. Clair Ellis and his wife, who was very wealthy. I did two portraits of Commander Ellis, one in uniform and one in civilian clothes. All his ribbons had to be just so. He wanted his eyes to have just the right sparkle – lively but dignified and stern.

I was just finishing the second portrait when the false armistice burst upon us. Everyone knew the real thing wasn't far off, and most of us applied for a discharge. To prevent a stampede, the Navy ruled that no honorable discharges were to be granted. All leaves were cancelled, too.

Well, I wanted to get out real bad. So, I told Commander Ellis that the only place in the Country where truly beautiful frames could be bought was Knoedlers in New York. 'I can pick out just the right ones,' I said, 'big, ornate, gold leafed. They'll make the portraits look marvelous.'

He sent an aide to look up the rules on discharges. The aide reported that under the temporary order prohibiting honorable discharges, there were only two ways to get me out of the Navy at once: a dishonorable discharge, or an 'inaptitude' discharge. 'Give him that inaptitude thing,' said Mrs. Ellis. 'Good Heavens!' said Commander Ellis. 'He can't go through life with an inaptitude discharge — What'll his friends say — that he's a moron?' 'Don't be silly, Mark' said Mrs. Ellis, and she worked at him until he consented to sign me out.

On November 12, 1918, one day after the real armistice, I was discharged as unable to adapt myself to the duties of a 'Landsman for Quartermaster' in the United States Naval Air Reserve

My service record reads: Discharged with Inaptitude — discharge. Rockwell is an artist and unaccustomed to hard manual labor. His patriotic impulse caused him to enlist in a rating for which he has no aptitude. Moreover, he is unsuited to Navy routine and hard work. And below is the terse comment: 'I concur in the above statement,' (signed) Norman Rockwell.

The next day I visited Knoedlers in New York and asked them to ship three of their gaudiest frames to Commander Mark St. Clair Ellis at the Charleston Naval Base.

COMMANDER MARK ST CLAIR ELLIS, U. S. N., AND MRS. ELLIS, whose marriage took place May 18, in San Francisco, surprising their many friends in this city. Mrs. Ellis was Mrs. Hugh R. Rood of this city.

Helen Allen Stoiber Rood Ellis
The Bonanza Queen

Portrait of Commander Mark St. Clair Ellis by Norman Rockwell

Chapter 26
Hansie

G wen moved once again to be near family; this time to the Berkeley area, where she remained for a year. She gathered up a groggy Hansie, now age eight, who was running a high fever. Her sister, Connie had arrived to watch the other children.

"Thank you for coming. Hansie is burning up with fever. I kept hoping that he would improve, but nothing I am doing has helped. Perhaps it's turned to pneumonia. It's this awful drafty apartment. Soon, I hope to be able to move to a decent home. This dreary damp place is not good for any of us, but I can't afford anything else right now."

Connie pressed money into Gwen's hand, "It's not much, but you will need some cash for travel. I'll say my prayers for Hansie."

"Thank you." Gwen left with Hansie in her arms. "I've left word for Henry to meet me at the hospital."

Located in Eldridge, California, The Sonoma State Home, for the care of children with developmental disorders, was available to all residents of the area. Originally opened in 1891, although plain and sterile, the rooms and the halls were well kept, and the floors were cleaned and polished daily.

Henry and Gwen sat together in the waiting room which was filled with other families waiting for word about their loved ones.

Henry had aged considerably and appeared pale and

downtrodden. No longer the smartly dressed gentleman, he looked shoddy, and his clothes were worn and ill-fitting.

He turned to Gwen, "I read the papers and hear the gossip. I want you to know that I would do whatever I could to help you." He shrugged and looked down at his feet, "The problem is my luck seemed to run out when I lost you. My restaurants failed, and I was forced to sell my properties to pay debts. Just recently, I had to sell our home, as well."

He sighed and continued with resignation. "So, you see, my dear, I am afraid that I am penniless."

Gwen dried her eyes and spoke with false bravado. "I'm truly sorry for your troubles, Henry. But, I should be fine once the court case is concluded. I can't do much, but perhaps I can help you out a bit once I receive my money. You've always been so good to me."

"That is very sweet of you Gwen, but you will need all your funds to support yourself and the children." He paused a moment. "You know I have never stopped loving you, Gwen."

She looked up through her tears. "Thank you for that. You're a good man. I'm glad you're here. Right at this moment, I feel more alone than I ever have in my life."

The doctor walked in. He was a distinguished gentleman in his mid-sixties with gray hair. He took a seat opposite them and removed his glasses. "I am so very sorry to have to tell you this. I'm afraid that his lungs were filled with fluid and he suffocated before we could do anything further for him." He paused. "I wish there was something more we could have done, but it was too late."

Gwen and Henry were distraught. Gwen buried her face in her hands and sobbed. Henry put his arm around her and hung his head, too heartbroken to even cry.

Chapter 27

1937—San Diego to Annapolis

Situated in a lovely community of homes just off the Severn River, the Atoll, as the house was named, was a white clapboard country home, surrounded by tall trees.

The interior of the home was finely furnished with antiques of European and Asian styles. In his study, retired Commander Mark St. Clair Ellis sat at his desk reading the letter he had just received from his daughter, Mary. He was a sturdily built, handsome man of sixty-four.

He stood, letter in hand, and walked from his study into the dining room where his wife, Rosa, was having coffee and reading the paper. Rosa was a former Italian countess, rather regal – a handsome, but not beautiful woman; her demeanor aloof. She looked up as he approached. "Rosa, my dear, I have just received a most interesting letter."

"Oh, really, from whom? "She sipped her coffee.

Mark poured himself a cup of coffee from the silver service on the sideboard and sat at the table. "It seems that I have been located by my daughter, Mary. You may or may not remember my telling you that she was adopted by a family in San Diego."

Rosa leafed through the paper and looked up occasionally. "Does she say for what purpose she is writing to you at this time? I would be wary if I were you."

Mark replied, "She seems only to want some answers to the changes that occurred in her childhood; what transpired between me and her mother. Understandable, I suppose. And, as well, she is interested in the whereabouts of her brother, Edward, and her sister, Rose."

She put down the paper and spoke pointedly, "Be careful of what you divulge. I think I would try to know more about her and her present situation before I would give out any information about yourself and others. You really don't know what her ulterior motives might be."

Back in his study, Mark returned to his desk. He was thoughtful as he picked up his pen and selected his letterhead stationery and began to write.

July 16, 1937
Dear Mary,

Your interesting letter has just been received and I answer it at once, but I shall reserve till much later the answer to your questions. Anyone as young and intelligent as you should not worry much about his or her origin.

I shall await with interest the receipt of your latest photograph and further details about yourself."

Respectfully, etc.
Mark St. Clair Ellis

Mary sat at her desk at the Gas and Electric Company reading the letter from Mark. She stood, letter in hand, and walked over to Ted's desk and read the letter aloud.

Ted commented sarcastically, 'Respectfully, et cetera?'

Mary rattled on in frustration. "He's simply answering my questions with more questions! He hasn't told me anything about my mother and why they didn't stay together. And he didn't mention my brother and sister."

She waved the letter. "And, he's asking me for a recent photograph, and to tell him more about myself. What? He's not going to talk to me unless I look pleasing to him?"

Ted rocked back in his chair and regarded Mary. "Mary - let's look at it from his point of view. The man receives a letter from out of the blue, from a daughter that he hasn't seen for over fifteen years. Maybe I'd be a little cautious, too. "He leaned forward. "Of course, we don't want to tell him what you're really like!"

"Very funny!" Mary walked back to her desk.

She picked up her paper and pen. and began to write: *If you are unwilling to share any other information with me about the past, then please do tell me of the whereabouts of my brother and sister.*

In his home in Annapolis, Mark sat at his desk reading Mary's return letter. He studied her enclosed photograph. There was no doubt that she was his child; he thought that she resembled his own family over that of her mother, Gwen.

Two weeks later, at the beach, Mary walked along the water's edge, Mark's letter in hand.

Dearest Mary,

Your letter came yesterday. To answer your question: no, I am not on duty at the Academy, I am married to Rosa, a charming European lady; we have a lovely home here of our own. We trust you will visit us here- But, only after you have read and fully understand what follows. If you can content yourself to call me cousin Mark when you come to see us, we shall be pleased to have you as our guest in our lovely home, in your capacity as 'the daughter of my very dearest deceased friend'. My wife is fully cognizant of everything and joins me in the invitation. We have been married but three years, and each of us has a nice income, but it dies with us.

…If you desire to see me, I may send you a round trip ticket with expense money to come, when you have a vacation. I think I can tell on sight of you, if you were my offspring. As mentioned in my previous letter, I will reserve, until later, the answer to your questions.

Meanwhile, may I not request that you use prudence in this regard and do not make any news notoriety which would preclude our further growing friendship and affection. Also, I ask that you fully inform your adoptive parents of our correspondence and projected visit.

Yours for Peace, Health and Happiness,
Mark St. Clair Ellis

Later, she sat up in bed re-reading the letter and mumbled to herself, "Does he think I'm just a gold digger?" Mary, her brow knitted, folded the letter, then tucked it under her pillow, turned out the light and prepared to sleep. "The daughter of your very dearest friend, indeed!"

Mary must have read over Mark's letter twenty times, but in the end, she wrote back to say that she would like to come to see him. When she received her ticket and travel money, she knew that she needed to speak with Mother and Dad Beeler.

At home, Mary entered the sunroom, where Gilbert was

reading his book and Edith was tidying up. "I need to speak with you both. I have something to tell you."

Edith bristled and Gilbert looked apprehensive.

Mary swallowed hard. "I have found out the true identity of my father. His name is Mark St. Clair Ellis. I've been in touch with him and he's sent me a ticket to visit him in Annapolis, Maryland."

Edith and Gilbert were speechless. Recovering from the news, Edith was infuriated. "Your father? That man has never shown one bit of interest in you in all these years! We are your family. Dad and I have raised you, clothed you, fed you, and this is how you repay us? You ungrateful, miserable girl." She marched towards Mary, her voice at a fevered pitch, "I'm sorry I ever wasted my time on such an ungrateful..." She raised her hand to strike Mary.

Mary caught her arm. "That is the last time you will raise your hand to me."

Edith Beeler was shocked and then she seemed to visibly de-flate. Mary turned and left the room. She had never stood up to Mother Beeler before. It felt somehow out of place and yet she knew, that ever after that moment, she would be free.

The next week Mary met with her boss, Ray Brown, in his office. "Of course, you must go to see him, Mary. But, how long do you plan to be gone?"

Mary shrugged her shoulders. "Including travel days, I guess that I should ask for three weeks off."

Ray smiled at her with a devilish twinkle in his eye. "It's a cruel world out there. Don't you think you better take along a traveling companion? Perhaps a charming, handsome, older man?"

"Oh, sure, Ray, I'm sure your wife would just love that one."

He answered brusquely, "Never mind my wife." His demeanor softened. "The time off shouldn't be a problem. We'll just have to hire a temp while you're gone. Not that you're replaceable!"

Ray gave her what the girls playfully called 'the hairy eyeball'. Mary rolled her eyes as she left the office.

In the end, there was nothing Edith Beeler could do. Mary had her tickets and her money. Edith did help Mary to get her travel wardrobe together, even though she was barely speaking to her. She said that she couldn't have them thinking that they hadn't taken care of Mary.

Mary had chosen a green velvet suit. The slim line skirt skimmed her hips and the jacket was sheared at the waist. Her hat was Empress Eugenie style with a veil and was worn tipped to one side in the style of the day. She planned to wear that outfit upon her arrival in Annapolis to meet Mark.

On the train platform, Mother Beeler stood prune-faced to say goodbye.

It took three days and three nights to get from California to Maryland.

Mary took the train from San Diego to Los Angeles. Then, she boarded the 'Super Chief', the first diesel-powered all Pullman sleeping car train in America, via the Atchison, Topeka and Santa Fe Railway. The train passed through eight states on the way to Chicago. The new train cars were heated and air-conditioned, and the accommodations on the Pullman cars were not only comfortable but luxurious. There was a lounge car between the sleeping cars where passengers could relax and socialize and observe the beautiful scenery as they travelled across the Country.

Mary was mesmerized by the region's beauty and allure. She was amazed at the grandeur as she travelled through the vast expanse of the Fabled American West; past the ranches, pueblos, mountains and deserts.

At times her mind would travel back through her childhood and then settle on how she came to be at this point in her life; traveling to see a father that she hadn't known since she was a small child. And then she was filled with both hopefulness and anxiety.

She was impressed by the vastness of the Country and the changing of the colors of each region; the subtle blues, golds and purples as she travelled through the northern part of Arizona, past the petrified forest, then through Albuquerque, New Mexico and the southeast part of Colorado. They passed the dense forests and farmlands of Kansas, crossing over the Missouri River, which separated Kansas from Missouri.

She saw the billowing cornfields and forests of Illinois, 'the Prairie State', and then rolled through northern Arkansas with its rolling forests and bluffs. Then on to Chicago where the train met up with the Baltimore and Ohio Railroad for the remainder of the trip.

Western Maryland was especially beautiful this time of year with colorful fall foliage of reds, ambers, and golden greens sweeping through the Allegheny mountain areas.

The Baltimore and Ohio train featured Colonial style dining rooms. The windows with their side panels and overhead ovals of leaded glass were of the Georgian style. The wall sconces were of pewter with crystal globes. Sitting in the dining car was Mary's favorite part of the trip.

The chairs were of Heppelwhite design and the tables were all set with starched white linens. Meals were served on the railroads' famous blue Stafforshire china.

Her favorite meal was at breakfast time where she enjoyed pots of steamy coffee served in heavy silver service, and cornbread slathered with butter and marmalade. Mary thought it all quite elegant, and she felt grateful to be enjoying this special trip. She realized that Mark had provided her with the best of accommodations.

The waiters all wore starched white uniforms and bow ties. Mary noticed that other passengers called each waiter George when addressing them. She thought that odd, and that evening at dinner, she spoke to her waiter, "Excuse me, waiter, but could you please tell me if all the waiters are named George."

He answered, "No, Miss. We's all called George, 'cause we works on the cars made by Mista' George Pullman."

Mary asked, "Do you all like being called George?"

"No, Miss, we don't, 'specially."

"Well, what is your real name, if I may ask?"

"My name is Isaiah, Miss."

Mary was thoughtful for a moment, "Well then, may I call you Isaiah?"

Isaiah smiled, "Thank you, Miss, I appreciates that. And what would you like for your dinner, Miss?"

The last morning of the trip, Mary sat staring out the window as the countryside flashed by. She was deep in thought. Meeting her father, after so many years, was both exciting and stressful.

The conductor announced the Baltimore Station. Mary checked her image in her compact mirror and refreshed her lipstick. She wondered, *Would he be pleased with her?*

Mary Ellis Beeler

Chapter 28
1937—Annapolis, Maryland

P enn Station in Baltimore was built in 1911 in the Beaux-Arts style architecture. As Mary entered the lobby of the station, she was struck by the light that streamed through the intricately designed stained glass ceiling. She collected her luggage and walked through the archways at the front entrance.

The Ellis's chauffeur awaited her at the entry to the station. Behind him was an elegant town car, and she thought it to be quite handsome. The chauffeur put her bags in the trunk, then held the car door for her.

It was fall and the leaves were changing. On the way she commented, "Coming from California, I've never seen deciduous trees before. This is just incredible, being surrounded by all this glorious color. I think I must be in heaven!"

A nod, but no comment by the Chauffeur.

Mary leaned forward. "Could you tell me about Commander Ellis? What's he like?"

The chauffeur answered, "You will soon see."

Mary sat back, resigned to wait. The trip took about an hour from the station to Annapolis.

They arrived at the Ellis home, a white clapboard residence, just off the water. The neighborhood was wooded and the home, which was set back from the road, had a landscaped stone walkway. The sun was shining that day and Mary could see glints of the river through the tall trees.

The chauffeur held the car door. Mary stepped out, then

walked up to the front porch. There were beautiful mosaics surrounding the front door. She straightened her skirt, raised her hand to knock, and hesitated. After all the years of searching and hoping, this was a surreal moment. Then she knocked.

Mark answered the door in his velvet smoking jacket. His wife, Rosa, an attractive woman with short stylishly coiffed brown hair, stood behind him dressed in a silk caftan, holding her long cigarette holder. She was the former Contessa Centano from Italy and had been prominent in Paris' smart set.

Mark took Mary's hand and escorted her into the foyer, a big smile on his face, "Mary, Mary, just look at you! Turn around, I want to see you."

Mark appraised Mary as she turned around. "You're lovely. But, not half as beautiful as your mother!"

Rosa glared at Mary, and with that look, Mary was instantly deflated. She knew from the expression on her face that Rosa was going to hate her. With her long cigarette holder, Mary thought of Rosa as 'Lucrezia Borgia.'

"Mary, this is my wife, Rosa."

"I'm very pleased to meet you. Thank you for having me in your beautiful home."

Rosa answered formally, "You are very welcome. Mark has been looking forward to your visit. We trust that you will be comfortable while you are here." Then, she turned and walked into the dining room.

Mark smiled, "Now, Mary, I want you to make yourself at home. Just go upstairs. First door on the left is your room with a bath. You'll want to bathe and relax after that long trip. We're due at the officers' club for lunch."

Then he turned and walked to the study. Mary looked around and saw that she was alone.

She thought, "Just like that, I've been dismissed." So, she climbed the stairs to her room.

The room was furnished elegantly. There was a carved mahogany four-poster bed, dressed in fine linens and a hand crocheted spread. The curtains were of a floral chintz fabric, and a chaise was covered in ice blue satin. The walls were papered in a pale blue and white striped pattern, and even though she felt strangely out of place here, Mary thought that the effect was charming.

An hour had passed, and she had almost finished dressing when there was a knock. She grabbed a robe when she heard Mark's voice. "Mary, I have something for you."

She answered the door, and Mark entered. He presented her with a tray filled with lovely pieces of amber and jade and exquisite handkerchiefs of linen and lace.

She exclaimed, "Oh, my. How perfectly wonderful. What beautiful gifts. Thank you, so very much."

He nodded, "I am pleased that you appreciate beautiful things."

Mary picked up the items admiringly, then set them down. "Do you think we might have a talk?"

Mark replied, "Let's save the serious talk for later, shall we? Let's just enjoy our lunch today. We'll be leaving in half an hour." Then he turned and walked out, closing the door behind him.

Just like that, she was alone again. He was, definitely, a man who was used to giving orders. She was anxious for answers, but she knew that the world could look bleak when she was tired. Tomorrow would be brighter after a good night's sleep.

They rode in the town car, driven by the chauffeur, to the Naval Academy Officers Club.

Mark turned to Mary. "Now, Mary. How shall I introduce you - my daughter? I can't very well do that."

"I thought we agreed that I was to be the daughter of your friend. Just call me your house guest or your niece or whatever you wish."

Mark deliberated. "Then, you shall be the daughter of my dear friend from California." Mary remembered how she felt when she first read those words in his letter. It was galling, but it would do.

The interior of Rugby Hall was filled with impressive furnishings, large leather sofas, and there was a massive fireplace. A trio played semi-classical music. Mark, Rosa and Mary arrived in the entry hall. Upon entering the room, the occupants acknowledged Mark with a nod or a wave. Mark carried himself proudly to the table. Mary was nervous; she would need to be mindful of her conversations.

Three young officers, Lieutenant Tom Bradley, Lieutenant Neil Young and Lieutenant (junior grade) Jack MacGregor arrived at the table. Mark stood. Lieutenant Bradley addressed Commander Ellis. "How nice you're here, Sir."

Lieutenant Young said, "Good to see you, Sir." Mark acknowledged the young men. "Hello, gentlemen. I see that you all want to meet my Mary from California. Mary, this is Lieutenant Tom Bradley. He's a French Professor here at the Academy. And this is Lieutenant Neil Young. Neil is a doctor at the Naval Academy."

Mary smiled, "Very nice to meet you all."

"And this is Lieutenant, JG, MacGregor."

Jack bowed to Mary, but his eyes remained fixed on her. "Edgar John MacGregor the third, but please call me Jack."

Mary blushed. "So nice to meet you."

Mark cleared his throat. "We'll be having dinner this evening at our home, to which you are invited. Then with a wry smile, "Except for you Dr. Young. You're a married man."

Lieutenant Young chuckled. "Right you are, Sir."

Lieutenant Bradley acknowledged the invitation. "I look forward to this evening."

Jack replied, "And I, as well, Sir."

Mary brightened at the prospect and glanced once again at Jack who smiled back at her.

Mark said "Please dress for dinner. Drinks at seven."

The men walked away, and Mark leaned over to Mary. "You know, Mary, I've always felt that Naval Academy graduates make the best husbands."

Mary beamed, "Oh, I think that Jack MacGregor is so handsome."

Mark stiffened. "He may be attractive, but he is Scottish and Catholic, and that's a terrible combination."

Mary sipped her drink and contemplated his words. She thought it a strange comment. It was obvious that he was trying to introduce her to 'the right men', but wasn't that her right to choose the one? She guessed, 'not according to the Commander!'

That evening at the Ellis home, before guests arrived, Mark showed Mary, drinks in hand, his collections in the living room cabinets that were filled with beautiful objects of jade.

"Oh my, you have so many beautiful things, Mark."

Mark waved his arm expansively to take in the room. "Everything in here will be yours. I'll leave it to you."

Mary eyed a crystal ball on a pedestal. "Please tell me about that crystal ball. It's just so intriguing."

Mark took a sip of his cocktail. "I was a young lieutenant

over in China during the Boxer Rebellion, and this fellow falls in the water, and he began yelling that he couldn't swim. So, I jumped in and saved him."

Mary looked at him, impressed with this news. "Well, that was very brave of you."

Mark nodded, acknowledging her compliment. "The sea was full of germs and afterward, I was all broken out in a rash. He happened to be an old Mandarin who was quite wealthy, and according to the Chinese custom, he said, 'You saved me and now my life belongs to you."

Mary was intrigued with the story. It was difficult not to be impressed with such tales.

"But, I said, 'Nonsense, I'm a Navy man, and that's what we're here for - to save people's lives.' Then he said, 'Let me give you something, and invite you to dinner.' While I was at his home, he offered me anything that I would like to have, and I said that I would like to have that crystal ball. I often find myself gazing into it. It's quite mesmerizing."

Mary admired the crystal ball up close. "It's just exquisite and it must be worth a small fortune."

Mark chuckled, "A man's life!"

Mary was quiet for a moment. "What was life like with my mother?"

Mark cleared his throat and held out his arm for her to take. "It's time to go into dinner, Mary."

She took his arm and they moved toward the dining room. Mary knew she needed to find the right time to speak with him, but that seemed to be an elusive effort so far.

The table was set with a beautiful lace cloth, fine china and crystal. Seated at the table on each end were Mark and Rosa. Seated on one side were Mary and Tom Bradley and across from them was Jack MacGregor. Rosa was deep in conversation with Tom Bradley.

Jack turned to Mary. "How much longer will you be here?"

He was flirting with her. Their chemistry was palpable. She was titillated but responded coyly, "My return reservations are in two weeks."

"Well, then, you must let me show you around the town of Annapolis. Perhaps a day of sightseeing and dinner might be nice." Jack turned to Commander Ellis for approval. "Of course, if that's all right with your hosts, Commander and Mrs. Ellis?"

Mark stiffened slightly. "I have many things planned for Mary while she is here. She'll have to let you know later."

Jack turned and grinned at Mary, and she blushed. "Thank you, sir. I'll be looking forward to that."

At home, later that evening, Mark was at his desk in his study.

Mary entered the room. "Thank you for a lovely day." She paused, then proceeded. "Mark, I'd really like to talk to you about my family."

Mark stood, "It's late, Mary, and I'm really tired. They'll be plenty of time for us to talk while you're here."

Mark left the room, and Mary was left staring after him.

She thought, *When will the time be the right time?* She was becoming frustrated. Was this trip just so that Mark might meet and appraise his daughter, without divulging any of the answers about her family? She didn't sleep well that night.

The next day, Mark was not feeling well. He left word for Mary that his friends, Captain William Little and his wife Laura, would be stopping by after breakfast to take her on a tour of

Baltimore. Mark said she would be pleased to know that Captain Little had known her mother, Gwen. Someone else who had known her mother! She could hardly wait for the day to begin.

William Little had been in Mark's command when Mark was active in the Navy, but now he had been elevated to Captain. Mary found both William Little and Laura very easy to be with, and she was soon at her ease. Of course she asked them if they knew what happened between Mark and Gwen, but, Captain Little said that he felt that it would be Mark's place to tell her about their life together. He did say that he found Gwen to be not only a great beauty, but charming and intelligent, as well. Of course, Mary was thrilled with his words.

The trip to Baltimore City took about an hour, and on the way, they chatted about what they had planned for her to visit on their day of sightseeing.

"First, Laura said, we thought you might like to drive past the residence of Wallis Warfield Simpson. The family had no funds of their own, so after her father died, Wallis and her mother lived with her wealthy uncle. And, of course, we all know now that the King of England abdicated the throne for her last year."

"Yes, I have been reading all about her. All of my friends were fascinated with her fabulous jewels and, of course, her great style with clothing, so that would be fun to see."

"And," Captain Little said, "You have a wonderful port in San Diego, so we thought you would enjoy seeing our Port of Baltimore. Then, we plan to have lunch at the Emerson Hotel. It has an interesting history."

"It seems that on one occasion, Isaac Emerson, the Bromo Seltzer king, was dining at the Belvedere Hotel. Although it was hot as Hades, and the room was not air-conditioned, they would not allow him to take off his jacket. So he said, 'The hell with this place. I'll build my own hotel' - and he did just that."

Mary laughed. "It must be amazing to have so much money that you could do something like that. What a character Mr. Emerson must have been!"

"If we have time, Mary, we'll visit Fort McHenry where Francis Scott Key witnessed the bombardment of the area from a British ship on which he was prisoner. It was then that he composed the lyrics of 'The Star-Spangled Banner', our national anthem, which we all cherish."

Sightseeing was great fun for Mary. When they visited the grave of Edgar Allan Poe, she remembered how his poetry always gave her chills. As a musician, she especially enjoyed visiting The Peabody Institute. But, most of all she was happy to be in the company of one who had known her beloved mother. It was a wonderful day.

Mary made a date to have lunch with Laura Little before she left for California.

Dinner that evening at home with Mark and Rosa was pleasant. The conversation centered around her impressions of Baltimore. She spoke about how nice it had been to spend the day with the Littles, and how very much she appreciated being shown the city. Rosa excused herself after dinner, and then, once again, Mark retired early.

She just sat there shaking her head and talking to herself. What was he thinking? She had come across the entire Country to find the answers to what happened to her family. And Mark continued to be evasive. She didn't think she could stand being put off much longer. She would find a way to press him for that conversation. Once again, she slept fitfully.

Jack had called the house to invite Mary to dinner. Mark had, begrudgingly, said that would be fine. For all his advice to Mary to seek a Naval officer for a husband, for some reason he didn't care for Jack McGregor. Perhaps he recognized something of himself in the young officer.

The next night, in the Officers' Club, Mary was seated at the piano. She played the melody 'As Time Goes By.' Jack leaned on the baby grand holding a drink. She completed the song, and the people in the room applauded.

The evening continued, and Mary and Jack enjoyed a romantic candlelit dinner in front of the fireplace.

Jack spoke sincerely, "I have to tell you how impressed I am, listening to you play the piano. I'm afraid I have no talent along those lines. The only thing I ever got from my year of practicing the trumpet was a swollen lip."

Mary laughed. "Well, if everyone played an instrument, there would be no audience to appreciate and applaud the performance. So, you see, you're a very valued part of the music world."

"I like the way you think, Mary Beeler." Then he smiled, "I'm going to take you sailing!"

Mary was delighted with the prospect of being on the water. "I can't think of anything I would enjoy more."

Mary and Jack had arrived on the dock at the Naval Academy. Mark could not very well object to her going for a sail. After all, it was certainly part of the local color.

They took one of the small twenty-six-foot sailboats that were available for the use of the officers and prepared to push off for a sail up the Severn River. It was a beautiful Indian summer day. The sky was clear and blue, and the sun sparkled like diamonds on the water. There was a flurry of activity as others prepared for a day of sailing, as well.

Mary had thought to pack her rowing costume since she knew that she would be near the water in Annapolis; nautical blue shorts and a white halter top with a wide sailor collar with a blue stripe border. She knew it was always colder out on the water, so she brought a lightweight jacket, as well.

"It looks like perfect sailing weather."

She gave Jack a salute, and then spoke in a flirty voice, "Aye-aye, Captain! Just give me my orders."

Jack untied one of the ropes from the moorings and threw it on the deck. He offered Mary his hand and she stepped on the boat. Then he followed and dropped the other rope on deck.

"Just take a seat in the back and I'll let you help me once we're underway. We'll be sailing towards the head of the river. There's a great little community of summer homes called Sherwood Forest, and they have a nice cove to sail into. It will be a good spot for us to stop for our picnic lunch."

Mary smiled, "That does sound lovely." She walked to the back and took a seat.

A few minutes out into the river, Jack hoisted the mainsail.

They headed west/northwest towards the head of the river. There was a good wind from the south/southeast.

Jack walked forward to the jib, the sail attached to the mainstay, and adjusted it to the wind by pulling on one of the control lines, and then wrapped it on deck. Mary's eyes followed his every move. She thought him so good-looking and loved watching his skillful maneuvering of the craft. After he secured the control lines, he walked back to sit with Mary. "The wind is ideal, and we are going on what is called a 'reach' up the river – otherwise known as smooth sailing.' We should be able to sail right on through the bridges with no problem."

She smiled, "It's just heavenly out here on the water. This was such a great idea." Mary felt the wind on her face and she was exhilarated. The water of the river had that mild fragrance of the bay that reminded her of her days of competitive rowing in San Diego.

"Now we'll put you to work, Mary." He showed her how to hold the tiller. "How about you hold the tiller midship, like this." She loved the feel of his hand on her own, and his closeness made her heart race.

The first bridge they came to, connected the southern shore and the northern shore of the river. It was a drawbridge, but being a smaller craft, they sailed under easily.

They sailed along in silence for a while. Mary wished they could go on this way forever. She found Jack so appealing that she was afraid to look at him for fear he would see the desire in her eyes.

Jack had his arm around Mary and he suddenly turned towards her and drew her to him and kissed her. "I just couldn't resist the urge to kiss you, one more moment. I'm sure that no sailor ever had a more beautiful first mate."

She grinned, "I'll bet you say that to all the girls."

He drew her closer and looked into her eyes. "No Mary, you're special."

"In what way am I special?"

"Well, you're smart and you're a great kisser. And you have great taste in men."

Mary laughed, "I do have great taste in men." He leaned over and kissed her once again.

The next bridge they came to was a trestle bridge and they waved to the operator who opened the bridge for them to pass.

They sailed into Round Bay. When they reached Sherwood Forest, a thickly forested area, they prepared to dock the boat.

Mary handed Jack the ropes and he dropped anchor and secured the boat. Sherwood Forest was a summer community, and according to tradition, all homes were painted green, and some were built on pilings.

Mary and Jack lounged on a picnic blanket. They sipped their wine and shared the sandwiches from the basket.

Jack held his glass high, "A jug of wine, a loaf of bread and thou beside me. It hardly gets better than this."

Mary grinned. Then she looked around at the shoreline. "I'd love to have a home on the water one day."

Jack looked over, "That would suit me fine."

She continued, "A friend once told me that there's nothing that can't be healed by the sea - not a broken heart nor a broken bone."

"Interesting thought." He paused a moment and became more pensive, "I received some sad news recently. My best friend, Ben, was killed in a car crash last month."

Mary was sympathetic. "How awful! You must be so sad."

"Yes, he leaves a young wife and a little boy of seven. They're coming for a visit in December. So, I'll be able to share some time with them while they're here. We've spent nearly every Christmas together, so it'll be really tough without Ben."

Mary reached out to comfort him, "I'm so sorry. It's not easy losing people we love." She looked up at Jack and touched his cheek tenderly.

He turned to her, "It certainly reminds us to make every day count."

Mary looked away. "It's so very beautiful and serene. I'd like this day to never end."

She thought about the recent days she had spent with Jack. He was always such a perfect gentleman. And there was that one evening while they were out dancing that a drunken lout had tried to force her out onto the dance floor. Without making a scene, Jack had grabbed the man and masterfully ushered him out of the building. Protecting her that evening, he had seemed her 'Prince Charming', for sure.

Jack kissed her hand and her heart was filled with love for him.

They returned to the Ellis home after dinner that evening. Jack and Mary sat on the piano bench laughing, while she played the piano, his arm around her.

Mark entered the room. He appeared miffed that Jack was still there. "It's a little late, Mary. We have a lot planned for tomorrow."

Mary stopped playing. Jack stood. "Sorry, Sir. I'll be leaving now."

Mary walked Jack to the door. He kissed her good night. She whispered, "Sorry."

Mary had managed to find a way to meet Jack most evenings. Since Mark was early to bed, he couldn't very well object to Mary going out after that, although he was disgruntled that she was spending time with Jack MacGregor.

On their fourth date, Jack proposed marriage. Life seemed more urgent when one was in the military. The possibility of combat was always imminent. "Mary, I realize that we haven't known each other for long, but the truth is, that I feel that I've known you all my life. I love you, Mary. Now that I've found you, I can't imagine my life without you. Will you do me the honor of becoming my wife?"

Mary clasped her hands together in joy. "Oh, yes, Jack! I love you, too. Of course, I'll marry you."

She was so thrilled that she could hardly sleep that night. It was late, and Jack stood outside throwing pebbles at Mary's upstairs window. After a moment Mary came to the window and looked out.

He waved a bottle of wine and spoke in a loud whisper. "Mary, come on down. Don't bring your bathing suit. We're going for a midnight swim!"

She laughed and turned away.

In the moonlight, Mary and Jack were in the water swimming nude. There was no one around and the full moon gave a lovely rippling light on the river. They came together, and he kissed her. She loved the feel of his body next to her own.

The water was brisk and her teeth were beginning to chatter, "Brrrr, I'm cold!"

"Well then, let's get you warmed up." They came to shore and grabbed their towels and ran for the blanket that was stretched out on the ground. Jack took her in his arms and hugged her vigorously, then the towel dropped. They kissed passionately and fell to the blanket.

Making love with Jack felt right, and she was filled with a sense of wonder at how naturally it had all evolved. As they lay there so close, she felt that there was nowhere else on earth that she would rather be than here in his arms, wrapped together in the blanket, looking up at the stars.

After a moment she turned to Jack, "I want to share with you the real reason that I came here for a visit." She paused. "I was hoping to find out some information about my family."

She sighed, "But, Mark's been rather evasive and I'm becoming discouraged."

Jack raised up on one arm and looked down at her. "Don't be disheartened. Just pin him down to a conversation. I can't imagine that he won't want to help you."

"You're right. I've come this far." But, in her heart she was not so sure that Mark would be forthcoming with her, and that was disappointing. She had been so hopeful.

The time had flown by, and the days had been filled with Mark's planned social gatherings for her. Then, there were the invitations from some of the young officers' wives to go to lunch in town. Meeting his friends had kept her on her toes so as not to say the wrong thing, and that certainly created a constant state of anxiety. She could feel her lips tingle and that signaled an outbreak of the 'dratted' fever blisters that were her nemesis.

As arranged, she did have lunch with Laura Little, and she shared her news of her engagement and of her love for Jack. She asked Laura that she not say anything to Mark until she had a chance to speak with him. Laura said that she hoped that she would be happy and that she would keep the news private as Mary had requested.

Chapter 29
The Conversation

The next evening after dinner, Mary knocked at Mark's door - her courage fortified with wine. They had spent a pleasant evening together at home, and even Rosa had seemed less stiff than usual. Mark opened the door.

"Mark, I've been here for almost two weeks now, and you have still not spoken with me about my family."

He waved her in the room. "Come in, Mary."

Mark motioned for her to have a seat. He seated himself, as well, drink in hand. "Aren't you having a good time?"

"It's not that, Mark. Of course, I am having a lovely time being here. But, socially, it's becoming uncomfortable for me, particularly when other girls from the area invite me places, and I don't know what to say and what not to say when I'm with them. Please, Mark, tell me what happened. What was it? Who am I to you?"

He regarded her calmly. "I thought we agreed that you're my friend's daughter."

"That's here and now. But, what happened between you and my mother? What happened to my family?"

Mark settled back in his chair, paused a moment, then began. "You put the case now so squarely up to me, that I am obliged to tell you what, I wished, could have been left untold for some time. I never was married to your mother, during all the period I knew her so intimately and loved her so much."

Mary sat back in her chair and listened.

"I fell madly in love with Gwen the moment I met her. All reason slipped away; she became my obsession, and I pursued her relentlessly. I was possessed. I simply couldn't help myself. She was so beautiful. We fell in love." He paused in thought. "Gwen used to tell me that she loved me like she loved God."

Mary was mesmerized by his words.

"She eventually got a legal separation from her husband, and we took up residence together. I tried to keep our relationship private. I felt guilty about my invalid wife who had been ill for years."

Mary sighed, "I see." His words gave her pause. They had both been married.

"Gwen and I found that we had many interests in common. Gwen was so much smarter than I. She could read the newspaper from front to back in the blink of an eye and she would know everything in it, while I was still concentrating on the front page."

Mary was wistful as she spoke, "We used to love it when she would read to us when we were little."

He leaned in towards Mary. "I loved your mother very much. We had three beautiful children together. And you were very much wanted by both of us." He spoke with a twinkle in his eye. "And, if you have my blood in your veins, you are a veritable 'enfant d'amour'. Such children are generally the smartest and the prettiest."

Mary ignored his feeble attempt at flattery.

He sat back in his chair. "My experience in a long life now, sixty-four years past, is that it is nothing to be ashamed of." His demeanor became reflective, "I was to sea much of the time. And, it was very expensive keeping two households. And Gwen was a very expensive woman."

He sipped his drink.

"When my wife, Elizabeth, found out about Gwen, she cut me out of her will completely. That was the money I had counted on to support your family. After Elizabeth died, I felt that the only way out of my dismal financial state would be to marry into wealth. So, when the opportunity presented itself to marry Helen, The Bonanza Queen, I took it."

Mary was taken back. "How could you marry someone else and leave Gwen with three children?"

Mark waved his arm in frustration to her response.

She pressed on, "And what happened to Eddie and Rose?"

Mark simply shook his head and sipped his drink.

Mary was incredulous. "That's it? That's all you have to say?"

"You're young, Mary. Life takes unexpected turns."

Mary was quiet for a moment. This was not what she had expected to hear. She needed time to take it all in – to realize the breadth of the abandonment of her family. Then she stood, "You know, Mark... I wanted to love you. I needed to love you. But, I'm having a hard time with that one."

She turned to walk away, then stopped. "I'll be leaving on the next train back to California." Then she left the room. Mark continued to sip on his drink and stare into space reflectively.

Mary had been able to exchange her return train ticket to one day earlier than originally planned. It was noon and she was on the train settling into her cabin. It didn't seem to be as crowded today, on the return train, as it had been coming from Chicago.

Jack ran frantically alongside the train and looked in the windows as he went along. He came to Mary's window, and he knocked anxiously. She looked up and saw him and her heart skipped a beat. She jumped up and walked quickly down the aisle and stepped off the train onto the platform.

Jack took her in his arms and kissed her. "I stopped by the

house and they told me you were leaving on the next train. Were you just going to leave without saying goodbye?"

"I'm so sorry, but, I decided to leave rather quickly. I tried to get hold of you, but you were unavailable. "I left a letter for you at the Officer's Club."

He stood and took her in his arms and kissed her. "We have plans to make."

"Yes, I know. But, I need to go back to California and speak with my family and tell them of my intentions. And then, I will need to notify my place of employment of my decision to leave. So, I will be busy these next few weeks. But, I will be holding you in my heart until we are together again. It will just take me some time to prepare. And then, I will be on the eastbound train to be with you."

On their last dinner date, they had decided to get married in the Naval Academy Chapel, just the two of them. Jack had said that his parents were divorced and with Mary's family situation, it seemed the sensible thing to do. And then they could notify friends and family of their union.

The conductor shouted, "All aboard!"

Jack finally let Mary go. She turned and climbed aboard the train and waved.

He hollered, "Take care, my darling. Write to me, often-- I'll be missing you."

She blew him a kiss and waved goodbye.

Chapter 30
Broken Promises

From articles in the San Diego Evening Tribune, Dec. 3, 1919:

PATHETIC STORY TOLD BY WOMAN
WHO IS NOW SUING NAVAL OFFICER

Mrs. Gwen Dierks told her story of her alleged relations with Commander Mark St. Clair Ellis in Los Angeles yesterday. It runs the gamut of human passions, of erring, trusting womanhood, and man's duplicity. Old as the tale is, as Mrs. Dierks told it, simply and without rancor, it carried the ever-new heart-twist born unfailingly when the woman, who has pinned her faith on a man and lost, lays bare her melancholy soul to the world's game.

It is her devotion to these children that has elicited the sympathy and admiration of those who know her, and it is for them that she is fighting, for their support and their future.

'I don't want him back,' she said, 'His conduct has killed all my love and respect for him. But I want a fair chance for his children, and it is his refusal to provide for them that has driven me to the courts in an effort to obtain justice, not for me but for them.'

From articles in the San Francisco Examiner December 2, 1919:

SAN DIEGO DIVORCEE' ALLEGES IN FEDERAL COURT THAT COMMANDER IS FATHER OF HER THREE CHILDREN

Mrs. Dierks says that she expected him to marry her and legitimatize their children, Eddie, age five, Mary, age three years and five months, and Rosie, age one year and seven months.

He kept putting her off, she declares, although he provided for the children and continued to do so, until May 1918, when without any warning to her, she says, he married Mrs. Helen Allen Rood, of Seattle, the wealthy widow of a Seattle lumber king who perished on the Titanic.

Mrs. Dierks says this marriage took place at the Palace Hotel, San Francisco, and that it was Mrs. Rood's fourth matrimonial venture. The present Mrs. Ellis, according to Mrs. Dierks, is the owner of the Washington Hotel and the Moore Theatre at Seattle, and maintains homes in Paris and Denver, the latter being one of the show places of Colorado. Immediately after this marriage, Mrs. Dierks says, Commander Ellis stopped providing for the children and has persistently refused to do so from that time.

She asks the Federal Court to compel him to allow her one-hundred-fifty dollars per month for their support in addition to five-hundred dollars, which she already has already expended, and five-hundred dollars attorney's fees. Mrs. Dierks is living at 1956 Front Street in San Diego in poverty. Her struggle to support her three children has become so hopeless, she declares, that she has been forced to appeal to the courts to secure aid from their father, who she asserts, is happy in the love of a rich wife – recently wed.

1919—SAN DIEGO NEWSPAPER ARTICLE

Inside the San Diego Tribune newspaper office, a young reporter sat at his desk typing his article. He had met with Gwen earlier at her home, and decided to tell the story in her words:

"It was in 1912; I separated from my husband and took an apartment in San Francisco, where Commander Ellis called on me as often as he could. Mr. Dierks, my husband, agreed to the divorce, but he was very bitter toward Commander Ellis, and declared his intention of naming him co-respondent and suing him for alienation of my affections. But I pointed out to him what that would mean to Commander Ellis's career in the Navy, and what it would mean to his invalid wife, at length prevailing upon him to allow me to get the divorce without scandal. My only thought was to protect my sweetheart. It has always been my thought, until now, and always has been his constant cry to me, to protect his name from being sullied, and his career in the Navy from being hampered. It was the one thing he seemed to fear. "

However, Henry Dierks went to Commander Ellis and exacted a promise that he would take care of her, getting a divorce eventually from his wife and marrying Mrs. Dierks. She says that Ellis agreed to do so.

"But despite his promises to me and Mr. Dierks, he refused to divorce his wife. He said that he could not bring himself to tell her, saying it would kill her. But I believe now, that the real reason was her property. She was worth about $35,000 and he expected to inherit it. Several times he told me that to tell her of our relations would mean the loss of this property when she died.

Nevertheless, despite his failure to keep his promise, I did not doubt him. He kept telling me to wait, to have faith and to wait. And I did. He was with me in the little apartment in San Francisco and we were very happy.

He paid for my divorce, and after a talk with my husband, he paid the expenses incurred with the birth of Edward, who came before my divorce was granted. He gave Mr. Dierks a check for $800, acknowledging by doing so, that the child was his.

Mary, our second child was born, and a third was expected, when the storm broke. His wife had discovered everything, and he implored me to leave San Francisco, immediately, to protect his reputation. He feared a scandal always, always thinking of his future. He could not bear the thought of our association becoming public knowledge. I agreed to his wish and went to San Jose where I took a little cottage under my maiden name, Davies.

This was two years ago, and I have never seen him since, although I have heard from him countless times. His wife died in February,1918, and did not even mention his name in her will, cutting him off absolutely, for which he had blamed me many times in his letters.

He continued to support me, in a fashion, and his letters still implored me to have faith, and to wait. And I did, still. I felt that to go to him so soon after the death of his wife would be bad taste, and I waited his convenience."

As she unfolded her Iliad of seven years from Vallejo, to San Francisco, to San Jose, to Berkeley, and at last, to the little cottage in San Diego, her three little children played at her feet - the children whose father, she says, is Commander Mark St. Clair Ellis, USN, recently married to a wealthy woman.

1919—INSIDE THE FEDERAL COURTROOM

Gwen was seated on the stand. She looked tired, drawn and haggard. No longer glamorous, her clothes were worn and drab and ill-fitting. Her attorney, Frank J. Macomber, interviewed her for the benefit of the Judge.

He turned and addressed the court "Mrs. Dierks is living at 1956 Front Street in San Diego in poverty. As well, she suffers with kidney disease. Her struggle to support her three children has become so hopeless that she has been forced to appeal to the courts to secure aid from their father."

He turned to Gwen who nodded. "Mrs. Dierks, will you please tell the court in your own words what has transpired?"

Gwen began; her voice was shaky. "It was in 1912 that I met him. During the six years of our relationship, we had three children together. All the while he gave me repeated assurances that we would be married once he was free."

She stopped and looked at the Judge. It took all she had to keep her composure. She was so humiliated to be in this dreadful position. "I don't attempt to defend my conduct. He made it seem very real, and I-- well you see, I loved him."

The Judge crossed his arms and sat back, seemingly unmoved.

Gwen cleared her throat and continued. "He continued to support me, and his letters still implored me to have faith. And, I did, still.

When I read of his marriage in the newspaper, the blow almost killed me. His utter faithlessness was too much to bear."

"He wrote to me and said, 'By your folly, I lost my marital inheritance, and the step I've just taken is the only thing left. If I play my cards right, all will come out all right. If you keep quiet it will be all right, otherwise, all is lost'. Now wasn't that a note to wring my heartstrings, coming from the father of our children who had, I supposed, been waiting his opportunity, for years, to marry me." Gwen hung her head for a moment.

"I went to Berkeley where I remained nearly a year, and still he supported me in a fashion, but when I left there to come down here, he stopped my allowance, although I came at his suggestion. Since last August, he has refused to contribute a cent toward the support of his children."

Attorney Macomber addressed Gwen, "With no means of support, how you have managed to survive?"

"My father and sister have helped me to live, although they could ill afford it. But my sister will soon be leaving for the East Coast and will no longer be here to help me." She sighed and then finished her words. "That's all. Here I am with three children who should have a fair chance."

The Judge leaned forward, his demeanor softened. "The court will always consider the plight of the children."

Gwen heaved a sigh of relief. "Thank you, Your Honor."

FAYETTEVILLE, ARKANSAS

Mark paced back and forth in the drawing room of his family home, a paper in his hand.

Helen, somewhat portly, but well dressed and bejeweled, entered the room and closed the door behind her. Mark turned to face her. "Yes, Mark. What is so pressing?"

He waved the paper in his hand. "I have just spoken with my commanding officer. It seems that Assistant Secretary of the Navy, Roosevelt, has demanded answers regarding the cloud surrounding Gwen Dierks and the children."

He showed her the letter which she read, and when she was finished, she handed it back to him. "I don't see that you have a lot of options. Roosevelt says that if the rumors are true, he wants you dismissed from the Navy. I suggest that you take the smart way out and retire early."

Mark considered her words. It looked as if he was about to protest, but he resolved not to, under Helen's stern gaze. "This is a bitter way to end my career."

Helen turned to leave the room. Then she looked back, "We're due at dinner in an hour."

While Mark was still on active duty in the Navy, Helen and Mark had rented an apartment at the Opera House in Fayetteville. Helen had jewels that she said belonged to the Empress Eugenie. When she left the Ellis family home in Fayetteville for the apartment, she dropped them in her bosom and recited scripture to protect them.

Then, they bought a home on the corner of Spring and Willow, and they lived there for a while.

When Mark read the letter of inquiry from Franklin D. Roosevelt, regarding his 'second family', he knew his days in the Navy, as an officer and a gentleman, were numbered.

He shook his head at the irony when he thought about the previous correspondence he had received from Roosevelt in 1919; commending him for his extraordinary bravery at the magazine explosion on Mare Island; recommending that he receive a medal.

After speaking to a friend in whose command he had remained for some time, it was suggested that he take an early retirement due to illness. In that manner, he would be able to retain his retirement benefits.

In October 1919, Mark reported for three months sick leave, and in January 1920, he was declared 'physically unfit for duty'. He was released from all active duty and placed on the retired list as Commander, United States Navy on August 6, 1920.

After Mark retired from the Navy, he built the front porch of their next home, 'Pisa Aiukli', on Mt. Sequoia, Fayetteville, to the exact dimensions of his last ship's bridge. He would pace on it, back and forth, and look down at the city's reservoir just below, and imagine the ocean. Mark sat on that porch when he wasn't sauntering around town, and he would be reminded of his years at sea.

NEWSPAPER ACCOUNTS

February 2, 1920

Vallejo Evening Times
ELLIS WILL FIGHT CHARGES BY MRS. HENRY DIERKS
Former Yorktown Commander Will Employ Counsel and Fight Charges

San Diego Tribune
WEALTHY NAVAL OFFICER FIGHTS LOVE SUIT

San Francisco Examiner
NAVY MAN TO FIGHT CHARGE OF PATERNITY

Mark St. Clair Ellis, Charged with Being Improvident Parent, to Fight Woman's Petition:

The first move of Mark St. Clair Ellis, reputed to be a wealthy Naval officer, to fight the suit brought by Gwen Dierks of San Diego to make him support her three children, of whom she claims he is the father, will be made in the Federal Court today. Attorney H.T. Morrow will move to quash the summons obtained on Ellis in New York on or about January 15.

Morrow will appear as special counsel for H.F. Pearl of 514-18 Humboldt Bank Building, San Francisco, being listed as lawyer for the officer. Morrow said that he was not familiar with the details of the remarkable case and declared, yesterday, that he did not know definitely if Ellis is still in New York. It will be claimed that the service of papers cannot be held binding, as in such cases jurisdiction cannot prevail outside the district of the court in which the suit was filed, namely, in Southern California.

In the complaint filed two months ago, Gwen Dierks asked that Ellis be ordered to pay $150 a month for support of the children until the suit comes to trial and the same amount thereafter. She also asked for $500 she had expended on them since July 1, and $500 for attorney's fees. The children are Eddie, Mary and Rose Ellis, ranging from one to six years of age.

When the strange case of an alleged illicit romance came to light, Gwen Dierks told a remarkable story, saying that the officer had recognized the children and supported them until July 1919. He *had married another woman in 1918, she stated. His Navy pay is in excess of $5,000 a year, she alleged.*

When news of the suit broke in all the papers, Helen suggested that they move to Europe. In February 1920, both Mark St. Clair Ellis and Helen Allen Ellis applied for passports, intending to travel abroad.

The suit against Commander Mark St. Clair Ellis by Gunevere Dierks, on behalf of Edward Mark Ellis, Mary Jane Ellis and Rose Ellis, minors, was entered into the courts on November 14, 1919. After several attempts to serve Mark with papers regarding the suit, he was finally located and served at the Biltmore Hotel in New York on January 15, 1920. Mark's attorneys responded with a request to 'quash' the case based on the fact of improper service to their client.

The judgement against Mark was dismissed, due to the fact that he was served papers in New York, instead of California where the suit was filed.

FINAL MEETING WITH THE ATTORNEY

Gwen spoke to Frank Macomber in his law offices, "We've lost the suit?"

Attorney Macomber answered, "The case has been dismissed due to a technicality. We had to track Ellis down in New York to serve him the papers. We had tried to serve him in California, where the case was originally filed. But, he had already left town.

Gwen was incredulous, "Is there nothing we can do?"

"I'm afraid we have no further recourse available to us since he is no longer in the United States. Shortly after he was served in New York, he left for Europe."

Gwen hung her head.

Frank Macomber replied, "I am truly sorry.

Eddie and Mary Jane

Hansie Dierks

Mary Jane and Georgie

Rosie and Mary Jane

Mary Jane, Rosie, Edward

Guinevere

ASKS U. S. COURT TO HELP CHILDREN

Gwendoline Dierks and three of her children, whose alleged father, Mark St. Clair Ellis, a ealthy naval officer, has been sued for their support. The legal battle over the youngsters be-ns today before a federal judge in Los Angeles.

NAVY MAN TO FIGHT CHARGE OF PATERNITY

Mark St. Clair Ellis, Charged With Being Improvident Parent, to Fight Woman's Petition

LOS ANGELES, Feb. 1.—The first move of Mark St. Clair Ellis, reputed to be a wealthy navy officer, to fight the suit brought by Gwen Dierks of San Diego to make him support her four illegitimate children of whom she claims he is the father, will be made in Federal Court today. Attorney H. T. Morrow will move to quash the summons obtained on Ellis in New York on or about January 15.

Morrow will appear as special counsel for H. P. Peart, of 514-18 Humboldt Bank Building, San Francisco, being listed as lawyer for the officer. Morrow said he was not familiar with the details of the remarkable case and declared yesterday that he did not know definitely if Ellis is still in New York. It will be claimed that the service of papers cannot be held binding, as in such cases jurisdiction cannot prevail outside the district of the court in which the suit was filed, namely, Southern California.

In the complaint, filed two months ago, Gwen Dierks asked that Ellis be ordered to pay $150 a month for support of the children until the suit comes to trial and the same amount permanently thereafter. She also asked for $500 she had expended on them since July 1, and $500 for attorney's fees. The children are Eddie, Mary and Rosie Ellis, ranging from 1 to 6 years of age.

When the strange case of an alleged illicit romance came to light, Gwen Dierks told a remarkable story, saying that the officer had recognized the children and supported them until July, 1919; since then he had married another woman, she stated. His navy pay is in excess of $5,000 a year, she alleged.

San Francisco Examiner
Mon. Feb. 2, 1920
page 11, col. 5-8 BEST COPY AVAILABLE

Chapter 31

1921—San Diego Cottage

Three years had passed since Gwen first learned of Mark's marriage and the abandonment of her and the children. Matt Lovett had remained her loyal friend through it all. He had narrowly escaped being reprimanded, as he had gone AWOL on several occasions to care for Gwen.

Gwen had moved with Matt to a cottage at 4836 Narragansett Ave, not particularly a good area in Ocean Beach, San Diego. The place was drab and sparsely furnished. Everything needed redoing and freshening up. Paint was peeling, and floors were scuffed and scratched.

They had lived together for some time, but then they had married quietly when she became pregnant with her fifth child, Georgie, who was now six months old.

She prepared the children to play on the beach; Edward age eight, Mary Jane age five, and Rose age three. Her neighbor offered to watch the baby while she worked. She looked tired and hollow-eyed, signs of her illness that were apparent.

Matt walked over to Mary Jane and Rose and kissed their heads. Then he went to Gwen and hugged her goodbye. "I have asked for an extended leave. You are going to need the help while you are sick."

Gwen took a deep breath. "That would be good if you could arrange it. I don't know what I'd do without you."

Matt leaned down and kissed her. "Take care of yourself. You know how much I love you. Please remember to take your medication - no skipping doses! And no more useless herbal remedies."

She had travelled north for two days and she was finally able to see a legitimate doctor at the Alameda County Hospital, but she wasn't offered much hope for her improvement. Her kidney disease was too far advanced. Mary would later recall the revulsion of emptying bedpans filled with blood.

She smiled weakly, "Goodbye, then. Hurry back."

Gwen had found work at The Beach Café. A small restaurant offering home cooked meals, serving breakfast and lunch. She walked with the children to work where she was a hostess, a position that allowed her to rest in between meal service.

After they arrived, Gwen prepared breakfast for the children. The three jumped up onto the stools at the counter. "Here you are, children; creamy coffee and apple pie."

Mary exclaimed, "Yum, my very favorite!"

Eddie and Rose chimed in simultaneously, "Me, too, me, too!"

Gwen smiled, "Eat up, my darlings. And then you can play on the sand dunes. Be sure to gather up a bouquet of the purple sand verbenas for your Mama."

Mary shouted with glee, "We will, Mama!"

Then Eddie followed, "We'll gather the biggest bouquet!"

And Rose chirped, "The biggest ever!"

That day at lunchtime, the restaurant was filled with customers. At one table two ladies, mid-fifties, sat gossiping, eyeing Gwen as she helped to serve a nearby table. Both Adeline and Eleanor were members of the Ocean Beach Women's Club.

Adeline, leaned forward, "Surely you have read all about the scandal involving our hostess, the infamous Mrs. Dierks?"

Eleanor answered, "Yes, I understand that she's been living with a man named Lovett, who is not her husband. They say he's an enlisted man in the Navy."

"Really? And where does she live?"

"On Narragansett Avenue, certainly a less than desirable neighborhood." Eleanor continued, "Some people just think that they can buck propriety."

"And look outside. The children are just running free on the beach all day, with no supervision."

They both looked in the direction of the children, who were having a glorious time, picking flowers and running free.

Adaline spoke softly, "Perhaps we should try to take some action for the sake of those children. The Ocean Beach Women's Club might be interested in hearing about this situation."

Eleanor perked up, "That's an excellent idea."

Chapter 32

1921—Narraganset Avenue

E dith Beeler stood on the front porch of the Narraganset Avenue cottage and knocked at the door.

After a few moments, Gwen appeared. "May I help you?"

Edith asked, "I wonder if I might speak with you about your daughter."

Gwen was hesitant but opened the door.

That evening Matt arrived home on leave. He was in the living room with the children. "Eddie, pick up your shoes."

Eddie looked up from the game he was playing. "You're not the boss of me. You're not my father!"

"Well, I'm here and I'm trying to help your mother."

Eddie spoke defiantly, "Well, I don't want you here!"

With that, Eddie picked up his shoe and threw it at Matt. Matt grabbed the shoe and chased Eddie around the room until he ran out the front door.

The girls adored Matt, but, Eddie being a little boy, resented another man in his mother's life.

Matt walked into the bedroom where Gwen lay on the bed. She looked tired and drawn.

"How are you doing, dear?"

Gwen waved her arm to take in the room, "This is such a shabby place, but I don't have the energy to fix it up. It's depressing." She sighed and shook her head.

Gwen stared out the window. "I had a visit yesterday from a woman named Edith Beeler."

"What did she want?"

"She came to see me to ask if I would allow her to adopt Mary Jane."

With a heavy heart, Matt moved to a chair next to the bed. He took her hand and stroked it.

Gwen continued. "She told me that she would be able to give her every advantage; education, fine clothes. I wanted to tell her to go to hell, but she seemed so sincere."

Gwen shook her head and threw her arms up in frustration, "How could I have made such foolish decisions in my life that it has come to this? That I would have to consider giving up one of my children?

Matt replied, "I do what I can, Gwen, but I am limited in my ability to offer you more."

She turned to him, "It's not your fault, but now I must consider what's best for Mary Jane. Maybe I won't be around long enough, myself, to help guide her as she goes through life. I might not always be able to tell her what to do, but, I could certainly point out what not to do." Gwen laughed weakly at the irony.

Then Matt said, "If Mary Jane was in a good home you wouldn't have to worry about her."

Gwen summoned her anger at the suggestion. "Certainly, Matt! It's not your child - that you could give her away so easily."

After a moment, Matt sat back in the chair, "But, perhaps it would be a good thing for Mary Jane."

Gwen became exhausted with the effort of the difficult decision.

Chapter 33
Alameda County Charity Hospital

G wen lived for another four years after she gave up Mary Jane to the Beeler family. They were difficult years and fraught with illness. She had lived with not only the debilitating kidney disease, but the heartache of having given up one of her children, no matter the selfless reasons. Two years prior, Gwen had moved back to the Oakland area. With the state of her failing health, she needed to be near the medical facility that offered care to residents that were in need.

One day, Eddie had come home from school and found Gwen unconscious on the kitchen floor. On February 23, 1926, after several days in the Charity Hospital, her health had continued to deteriorate and Gwen, age thirty-nine, had died. The nurse on duty closed Gwen's eyelids and crossed her arms over her breast.

The priest stood with the children beside the bed. Eddie and Rose were both stricken. Their lips quivered. Eddie asked, "She's dead?"

A kindly man, the priest answered, "Yes, Eddie. I am so sorry. Your dear mother fell into a coma and she is now with God. You will want to say goodbye to your mother." Both children started to cry.

Eddie bent down and kissed his mother's cheek, lay his head on her chest and put his arms around her. Tears streamed down his cheeks; his face showed his grief. Rose hugged her mother's hand and sobbed.

The priest patted Eddie on the shoulder. "Eddie, you must be strong for little Rose." Eddie looked up at the priest, who asked, "Do you have any family here?"

Eddie answered tearfully, "No."

"Then, I will speak to the Holy Sisters and they will be able to help."

On August 28, 1926, the summer after Gwen's death, Matt Lovett delivered both Edward, age twelve, and Rose, age seven, to The Day Home of the Sisters of The Holy Family in Oakland, California.

Matt stood at the entrance and had spoken privately to the nun in charge. "Their mother has died, and their father is unavailable to them. I believe that the sisters have helped in their care while their mother was ill. I leave for sea duty tomorrow and they have nowhere else to go."

He hugged Rose and patted Eddie on the shoulder "Goodbye, children. I am so sorry about your mother. I know that you will miss her. I will miss her, too. I will try to come to see you when I am on leave. I know that you will be well cared for here."

Then Rose started to cry, "But, what about Georgie?"

"Georgie will go to live with my family."

They both kissed Georgie goodbye. Then Matt took his young son and left.

August 18, 1927
Sister Helena, Superior
The Roman Catholic Orphanage
Bay View and Newhall Street
San Francisco, California

Dear Sister Helena:

Am sending the following information concerning the family data on the two Ellis children. Rose, the child who has been with you since August 28, 1926, and Edward are the children of Mark St. Clair Ellis and Guinevere Dierks. The parents were not married. The father is said to have held a position of rank in the U.S. Navy, but was discharged from the service at a time when complaint was made regarding his association with Mrs. Dierks. The information at hand states that this action took place in San Diego and that the record of the San Diego Associated Charities had complete detail. The third child of this union is said to be adopted by a Mr. and Mrs. Beeler, San Diego.

The mother later married a man named Lovett and lived in Oakland. They had one child. The mother died at the Alameda County Hospital on February 26, 1926, and Mr. Lovett sent Rose and Eddie to the Day Home of the Sisters of the Holy Family in Oakland and left instructions that they were not to return to him.

The Holy Family Sisters had been caring for these children during the illness of the mother, who requested that they be baptized. As far as the records shows, I do not find that any of the relatives belonged to the Catholic faith. Since the death of the mother, the Sisters have been supervising Eddie and Rose and as they do not have accommodations where the children might be kept permanently; Rose was placed at The Roman Catholic Orphanage Asylum and Eddie has been boarded in a private home; the Holy Family Sisters have been paying for the support of the boy. Those Sisters know the family history and at a visit to this office about a month ago, Sister Superior was interested in getting Eddie placed in a boarding school.

Sister, at that time, said that she would like to have some of the relatives interviewed, but there has been no further message about this. A man named Owen Davis, employed as a detective at the Wells

Fargo Bank, is given as the maternal grandfather of these children, but he has a way of disclaiming this relationship, although at one time he was married to the mother of Guinevere Lovett. He is friendly with the boy but will do nothing about his support.

If you wish me to look into this matter further, Sister, I shall be glad to do so.

Yours truly,
Julia Daly

Chapter 34

1926—The Old Maison, Louis the 13ᵗʰ, France

For many years after his retirement, Mark lived abroad, principally in England, France and Italy.

In France, The Old Maison Louis XIII, purchased by Helen and Mark St. Clair Ellis, was located six and one-half miles from the Arch de Triumph, Paris, and five hundred metres south of the Monument to the Escadrille La Fayette. The home had four stories and Mark commented on 'the perfect architecture of the original Louis XIII Maison– pretty as a flower'. There was a lovely sun parlor and the small trees surrounding the outdoors were rhododendrons. One tree to the left of the castle was a cypress that was seven hundred years old.

Mark's studio was a separate building that was once the hunting lodge of Louis XIII. The room to the left, Mark said, was perhaps the oldest bathroom in France. The main room on the left was his bar with Pilsner beer on draught, where he laughingly noted he drank and prayed for the revocation of the Volstead Act, and the end of prohibition back home.

There was a cave of Henry III, that used to be three hundred yards long. It was now large enough to hold four thousand bottles of choice wines and liquors and the ancient key to the cellar measured over one-foot long.

They had three dogs, Dolly, Benno and Bella, that were champion boxers. Mark thought them the finest dogs in the world. He jokingly bragged that Benno spoke four languages. The dogs were cared for by a young man, Ramon, who was dressed in proper livery.

It was the cocktail hour and Mark and Helen had drinks in the drawing room. The three boxer dogs lay at Mark's feet. Helen leafed through a magazine.

Mark commented, "Tomorrow, I have been invited to go horseback riding with our neighbor, Marie Amalie, the former Queen of Portugal. Did you know that she was of French Royalty?"

Helen spoke, absently, "Really?"

Mark continued, "Yes. She was the daughter of Count de Paris, pretender to the French throne."

Helen, unimpressed, "Interesting."

Mark continued his chat, "I have a small painting that I think she will enjoy. So, I will invite her back here for drinks and present it to her then. It's part of that large collection that I purchased last month."

Helen murmured, "That sounds like a nice gesture."

Mark considered his next words, "The Navy Department has informed me that Gwen Dierks has died. They tell me that Edward and Rose have been sent to an orphanage."

Helen closed the magazine. "Oh, for God's sake, Mark! Is there no end to this saga?"

Mark's demeanor became introspective and resigned, "I suppose that in light of all that has transpired, and all that I denied previously, I have no choice but to send back word that they have contacted me mistakenly; that I have no children."

Helen smacked the table next to her. "And let that be the last of it!"

Mark assumed a pleading posture, "Still, I would like to provide for the children. We have so much, Helen. Can we not send the funds to see that they are cared for and educated? Surely there's a way."

Helen's eyes narrowed. "Oh, I see now. We've had this discussion before. Did you marry me only for my money? Was this just a marriage of convenience for you, and was I to be the soft touch to support your illegitimate children? Well, think again, Mark Ellis. Before this situation became public, I agreed to provide for the children. But, now, if you persist in this effort and humiliate me, make no bones about it, I will divorce you and you will be left with nothing. You best think twice before pursuing this and going against my wishes."

Helen straightened her back and threw back her head, "Humpf!" Then, she turned away and opened a book.

Defeated, Mark went back his drink. He petted the dog next to him. After a moment he looked up, "I must say, these three dogs are the most handsome of specimens. It's probably because they receive such excellent care, and it certainly shows." He rubbed the dog's ears affectionately.

THE OLD MAISON LOUIS XIII

PARC MARNES-LA-COQUETTE, SEINE-ET-OISE, FRANCE

Property of Mark Saint-Clair-Ellis

Six and one half miles from the Arch of Triumph. Paris
Five hundred metres south of the Monument to the
Escadrille La Fayette.

Chapter 35

1937—Ocean Beach

Mary arrived back in Ocean Beach after her time away in Annapolis. She stood on the porch with her suitcase in hand and tried the door. It was locked. She fumbled for her key, opened the door, picked up her suitcase, and stepped inside. Edith Beeler entered the room.

Mary said, "I'm home."

Edith said, "I see that." Then she turned and walked out of the room.

Mary was left staring after her.

Life slowly returned to normal at the Beeler's home. They didn't ask about her time in Annapolis and Mary didn't speak about it except that she did say that she had met someone special. That was all that was said.

It was just before Christmas and packages had arrived for Mary from back East.

At the Gas and Electric Company, Mary sat at her desk reading Mark's latest letter:

My darling baby, you will never know how sad I was to see you go. I wanted you to have no unpleasant moments here, but we all tried to do too many things.

I think for now that you are too young to marry. Better look them over for a while and meantime go ahead with your night school and make yourself valuable. No luck comes from hectic parties such as yours with Mr. MacGregor. I learned that he had absorbed an extra bottle of my strong red wine the other evening. My waiter tells me this happened after I left the table. Such fellows are not for my Mary.

Don't fail to exercise your body. Try to be as nice as you look.

Darling, I am just as proud of you as my father and grandfather were of me after graduating from this wonderful Naval Academy; only more, for your blood has told, although deprived of the priceless heritage I had in pride of ancestry and family.

We have seen nothing of the young philanderers who pursued you here. We learned that MacGregor and Miss Whomever were at the Club at a very late hour on Saturday.

Anyhow, I want you to take your time before deciding to marry. And I don't want you to marry anyone in the Navy below a full Lieutenant.

I am making up some nice things in a vanity bag to send to you. They are the last remnants of our glamorous life abroad. Two of our friends leave shortly for San Diego and I may give them a letter to you, but you must assure me that you will not weep and tell sad stories of your life and make them feel sorry for you. Nobody likes people they feel sorry for.

Mary thought he sounded like a pompous ass in one moment, stipulating who she should marry, and then reprimanding her for her feelings in the next breath.

The next week, each evening, Mary sat at a classroom desk, studying at business school. She had decided to continue with the classes and finish the business course she was taking.

Mark's last letter had been full of fatherly advice: She was perturbed at the comments about Jack and she had crumpled the letter.

At work at the Gas and Electric Company, the office was decorated for Christmas. Mary had received Jack's picture in his uniform with his hand on his sword. She was so proud.

She walked back to Ted's desk and held up the photo for him to see. She beamed.

"Here's a picture of my fiancé, Lieutenant, JG, Edgar John MacGregor, the 3rd! Have you ever seen anything so dashing in all your life?"

Ted looked at the photo. "I will admit, he's pretty dashing."

"Yes, and his Christmas presents just arrived, and they are so special... A beautiful scarf in all the fall colors. He remembered how I loved the changing colors of the trees."

Ted threw back his head, "My God - the girl's gone! Are we going to get any work out of you, now that you're floating around on cloud nine over lover boy?"

Mary giggled, "Maybe - maybe not!"

Then she leaned closer, "Mark keeps sending me letters full of fatherly advice."

Ted commented, "A little late, wouldn't you say?"

Mary whispered, "I really think that he's jealous of my relationship with Jack."

Ted said facetiously. "Really? Well, we're all jealous of Jack. He's so dashing, so charming."

She laughed. "And I'm sure that he'd just die if he knew we were engaged."

She clutched the photo of Jack to her bosom. Then she grinned at Ted and started singing the popular song of the day,

I'm putting all my eggs in one basket, I'm betting everything I've got on you. She giggled and returned to her desk.

The next week, as she walked to her desk, the mail clerk arrived and handed her a letter. Mary called back over her shoulder to Ted. "It's probably from Jack."

She opened the letter and read it and slowly sank into her chair. There was a newspaper clipping enclosed. Her hands shook as she opened it and read the words. She was in total shock. The paper hung in her hand. Ted came by and stopped short when he saw the look on her face.

She said, "It's from Captain Little."

She handed him the letter to read.

Mary dear,

Laura has asked me to write to you. We are terribly sorry to have to tell you this. It seems your beau, Jack, while in an inebriated state, has married his friend's widow.

I am enclosing the newspaper announcement. Please take care and do try to remember that all things happen for a reason, and often for the best.

Sending our good wishes to you,
Captain Little

Ted shook his head and handed her back the letter. He put his hand on her shoulder, "Come on, Mary. The boss is away. Let's just get you an early Christmas drink."

Ted took Mary by the hand and led her into the party room. He poured Mary a stiff drink.

She drank it down in one gulp. Then she hung her head and cried. "How could this happen, Ted?"

"People do crazy things. And that man's a real fool. Sometimes if it seems too good to be true, it's too good to be true. You don't need that kind of guy."

After a moment Mary straightened up. She took a deep breath in resignation. "I'll take another drink."

"Take it easy, Mary. Are you going to be okay?"

She nodded. He refreshed her glass. "I have to finish a project that's due. I'll be back in a little while."

Later in the afternoon, the party was in full swing. Mary had managed to have several drinks in a row, trying to drown out the painful reality of her lost love. At this point, she was drunk and systematically kissing all the men in the office. Most of the men took her antics in stride, but the women of the office raised their eyebrows.

Ted came back after his work was finished and seeing Mary totally inebriated, he said, "Mary, I think it's time to go. Let me give you a ride home."

Mary answered, slurring her words, "No, Ted. Am having a lovely time."

Ted spoke sarcastically. "Yeah, Mary. I can see you're having a great time."

Just then one of the male employees stopped by. "Hey Ted, don't take her home yet. I haven't gotten my hug and kiss."

Ted waved the men away and helped Mary on with her jacket and held her steady as he led her out of the office, "Sorry, fellas. It's time to go."

Mary stopped half-way down the hall. "You know, Ted, there's always somebody that wants to stop me from having a good time. First Mother Beeler, and now you. I'm sick and tired of being told what to do." She shook her finger at him. "You're like an old mother hen. You're just an old party poop. Just because you're stuck at home with no way to kick up your heels, you don't want me to have any fun either."

Ted took the dig and brushed it off as gibberish.

They arrived at the Beeler's home and Ted helped Mary out of the car. She was none too steady, so he walked her to the door. "You only knew the guy for two short weeks."

"Two of the most wonderful weeks of my life. Oh, my God, I'm so miserable."

She hung her head and cried.

Ted told her, "Maybe it's better to find out now that he's a cad than to waste a lifetime on someone like that. You can do better, Mary. You deserve better. Someone you can trust."

Mary stopped crying and began to laugh, "Well, when they're too nice like you, they're boring."

She laughed again and turned to go inside. Ted turned to leave, wounded.

Edith Beeler came out in her robe and witnessed Mary being poured in the door. Mary, teetering on her heels, raised her hand in a wave. Slurring her words, she threw out, "Good night, Mother Beeler. Don't let the bedbugs bite." Then she giggled and tried to weave her way to her room. Mother Beeler stood there, disapproving.

That next morning, Mary lay in bed crying. She was still in the office clothes from the night before, and she suffered with a monumental hangover – but, nothing was as hurtful as the loss of her darling fiancé, Jack. She had been so overjoyed with the prospect of her life with Jack, that even her disappointment in Mark had become less important.

It was Christmas Day. All the girls in those days wore fur jackets.

It was warm during the day but cool at night. Muskrat shrugs were all the rage and Mary had been told that she was to be given one for Christmas. But she wasn't given any gifts, and no one at home spoke to her all Christmas day. Even Dad Beeler didn't talk to her.

Mary returned to work after Christmas and knew that she would have to face everyone in the office and apologize for her drunken behavior. She walked over to Ted's desk. "Thanks for seeing me home. I guess I was pretty drunk. I hope I didn't say anything too embarrassing?"

"Well, since you've always said I was a nice guy, does that mean you think I'm boring, too?"

She was embarrassed, "Oh no, Ted! Don't be silly. I think you're just wonderful. I'm so sorry. Please don't be mad at me. I just couldn't take it." She started to cry.

Ted stood and patted her on the shoulder. "That's alright, Mary, I understand. There, there. It's not the end of the world."

"It feels like it to me. That's what it is. It's the end of the world."

Ted tried to comfort her, "You know you always have me, Mary. I'll always be your friend."

Sniffling, Mary dried her tears. "Oh Ted, that's very sweet of you to say. I'm truly grateful for your friendship."

Ray Brown, back from vacation, called Mary into his office. She stood at the doorway. Ray indicated for her to sit down. His demeanor was stiff. "Mary, I understand that your actions at the office party were rather disgraceful. I've been told that you had much too much to drink, and that you then proceeded to fall into the arms of all the men, both single and married."

She heaved a sigh. She had been told about her loose behavior by one of the other girls who tried to laugh it off. "I'm sorry. I've had a difficult time recently. And I guess I just let my emotions get the better of me. I assure you that it won't happen again." She stood to leave.

Ray Brown stood and walked over to her and tried to take her in his arms. "Well, perhaps all is forgiven if I can get 'my' Christmas kiss."

Mary pushed him away and backed off. "That's it! I've had just about enough of you two-faced men in my life!" She turned to leave, but she spun back around to face Ray, "Interesting isn't it, how you, yourself, seemed quite ready and willing to disgrace me a number of times before this?

Ray was speechless.

Mary continued, "You asked me if I had anything to say? Well, hear this. I quit!" She turned and left the office.

Later that day, she told Ted that of all the crazy things, the president of the Gas and Electric Company asked for her to play the piano for his holiday party. Apparently, the gossip of her previous drunken behavior had not reached his office. This was quite a coup, so instead of being fired, she received a raise. But, at that point, she had already decided that she was leaving, in any event.

She settled back into her life in San Diego; work and school and getting together with her special girlfriends from college. Then, there was the occasional concert at which she was invited to perform.

She had concluded that there would be no further input from Mark regarding her family, and she would have to live with that. She did stay in touch with him and was always interested in reading his letters, and grateful when he sent her extra funds. She tucked them away for the day that she could afford to live on her own.

Chapter 36
1938—San Diego to New York

M ark had found the whereabouts of both Eddie and Rose, and after some association with them, decided to share the information with Mary, but only under certain circumstances. He, of course, would need to control the situation.

Mary sat on a park bench reading a letter from Mark:

January 3, 1938.
My darling Mary,

I am pleased to tell you that I have located your brother and sister They are living in New York City. As for Rose, she is as pretty as the heather, well educated in a convent. She works at Bonwit Teller. Edward is an engineer; a bright handsome fellow, six feet four. Both take name of Fairbanks; the name of their foster mother at some point. I am enclosing their photographs.

Mary took out the enclosed photographs, then clutched them to her bosom.

She was barely five years old when she was last with them. But, she could see the memory of her mother's face in Rose, and she thought that Edward looked exactly like his father, Mark. She was overcome with joy.

She continued to read the letter.

I made a copy of your photograph which I have given to them.

Evidently, they had written to you many times over the years, but they never heard back. Please don't attempt to contact them until we speak. I will give you their address at that time.

Love,
Mark

Mary, incredulous, spoke aloud. "Don't attempt to contact them?"

Without waiting for Mark's approval, she wrote a letter to Rose at the Bonwit Teller Department Store, to tell her that she had finally found their whereabouts.

After that, she checked the mail at the office each day. Would Rose receive the letter? Would they even want to hear from her? After two agonizing weeks, just when she thought she couldn't stand it another moment, a letter came back saying that they would love to see her.

Back home in the sun room, Edith and Bert Beeler were talking about pruning the fruit trees in the back yard, when Mary entered the room.

"I have something to tell you both." She took a deep breath then continued. "I have found my brother and sister, and I'm going to leave to be with them."

Edith shouted, "What do you mean you are leaving? You're not going anywhere!"

"I'm not asking your permission, I'm telling you that I am leaving!"

Edith stood mouth agape. Mary turned and left the room.

It took her some time to prepare to leave home. When she was ready, she wrote back to Rose to say that she had bought a ticket and would be arriving from San Diego in two weeks at Grand Central Station. She wrote she would be thrilled to see them after all this time. Then, she gave her notice at the Gas and Electric Company.

It was a bittersweet moment for Ted. "Of course, I am happy for you, Mary, but I will miss you terribly. The office will not be the same without your presence. Stay in touch and come back to see us when you return to California."

In her room, Mary packed a suitcase. She was elated and hummed a tune. During the past year, Mark had been sending her money to be the 'best-dressed girl in town,' but she had been putting it all away.

Through a fellow musician who had played bass for her piano concerts, and had recently moved to New York, Mary had been offered a job to play the piano at the Warwick Hotel. She planned to stay at the Barbizon Hotel for Women until she became settled.

Once again, no one at home was speaking to her. She packed her bags and put away clothes she had decided not to include. She checked her travel papers, then put them in her purse.

She told Mark that she was leaving for New York. The train made a scheduled layover in Washington, D.C., before going on to New York, and Mary had agreed to meet Mark for brunch.

In the sun room, Edith Beeler sat concentrating on her knitting. Gilbert Beeler stared out the window. Mary entered, suitcases in hand. She put the bags on the floor and stood straight. "Mother Beeler, I have just one question. How could you have kept the letters from my sister and brother from me?

Edith, who sat tight-lipped, put down her knitting, and assumed a defensive posture. Gilbert Beeler was all ears. "Because they had no right. We adopted you and we were your mother and father, and Bert was your brother, not them. You were my little girl!" Her lip quivered, "I'm the one who raised you and took care of you and cared about you for all these years."

Mary was quiet for a moment. "If you expect me to understand your actions, I don't. I know there have been times in my life when you've been kind to me. I remember when I was a child and very ill, you nursed me back to health. I never could understand how you could be kind at one time, and yet beat me at another. But, this is the cruelest of all. How could you let me suffer and wonder what happened for all these years?"

Edith Beeler, with downcast eyes, replied, "You would have left."

There was silence and Mary shook her head. "I'm leaving today for New York. Goodbye, Mother Beeler." Mary looked over at Gilbert Beeler who was stricken. "Goodbye, Dad Beeler"

She picked up her suitcase. "I have to go now. I'll write to you when I get settled." She turned and left the house.

Mary arrived in the Washington, D.C. station for the layover. She stepped off the train and, as arranged, she took a taxi to The Hay Adams Hotel. Mary recognized that Mark always opted for the most stylish places to dine. But she couldn't help but contemplate that it would have meant so much to her young family to have been cared for all those many years ago.

She arrived at the hotel and stored her bags with the bell captain, and walked to the dining room.

At the table, Mary watched as Mark finished his plate of grilled sweetbreads. He carried himself with the same aloofness that she had grown accustomed to during her stay at his home.

The meal completed, they continued their conversation over coffee. "Mary, if I could have done anything differently, I would have done so. If it weren't for the damn lawyers, everything would have been alright. I had spoken with Helen about Gwen and the children, and she had promised to settle a substantial sum of money on each child. I thought that Gwen would be happy."

Mary was dumbfounded. "How could you think that the money would matter to Gwen if she loved you?"

Mark glossed over her comment. He seemed to sit up straighter in his chair; stiff and haughty.

"I was away and before my letter about the proposed financial arrangement reached Gwen, she picked up the paper and saw where I had married Mrs. Rood; instead of waiting for any word from me, she went to see a lawyer."

Mark continued, oblivious of Mary's withdrawal. "I kept sending her letters saying, 'please let me explain,' but instead she kept giving them to the lawyers and talking to the newspapers."

Mary sat back in her chair and crossed her arms. She thought that he must not think her too swift, if he thought that she would swallow his weak excuses.

He continued. "Then, I had to contend with Helen who told me… 'If you admit that you are the father of these children, you'll be disgraced, and you'll be thrown out of the Navy, and I will cut you off without a dime. Then what are you going to do'? 'Never let the heart manage the head' was always her sentiment."

Mark's shoulders slumped in resignation. "So, I simply said, 'I have nothing to say, no comment.' And after that I got drunk and stayed that way, …just didn't think, and stayed drunk. And when Helen and I divorced, I married Rosa."

Mary remained implacable; not a hint of sympathy in her eyes.

After a moment, she spoke with steely reserve. "You turned your back on your family."

Mark was taken aback, "I keep trying to explain to you! I would have suffered financial ruin, and everything I had worked for all my life would have disintegrated to nothing." He assumed a defensive posture. "When you are an officer in the Navy, you are not allowed a whisper of a scandal, or you are ousted without a penny and stripped of your rank. Can you not understand what that would have meant?"

Mary leaned forward. "Oh, yes, I understand. I understand that you simply took the path of least resistance, without any concern for the welfare of your family. That you allowed your children to be separated. That you could've saved Gwen when she was ill. That you could've saved me from a life of hell!"

She was quiet for a moment. "Well, that is just so poor. That's just so disgusting; it's so unfathomable that anyone could behave so selfishly."

His voice became authoritative. "Have you quite finished?

Mary was silent and simply stared at him.

Still haughty, Mark sat back. "I had no choice; my hands were tied."

Mary was incredulous. "Do you take me for a fool? I may be young, but I'm not stupid. What you did was without honor. And speaking of fools, I can see now that it was Gwen who was the fool - a fool for believing in you, a fool for love."

She was silent for a moment. She wondered how anyone could be so cold and calculating.

Mark became uncomfortable in the silence.

Mary spoke without looking at him. "But oddly, it is you for whom I feel sorry." She looked back at Mark. "You could've had it all, and you just didn't see it."

After a moment, she folded her napkin. "Thank you for lunch." She stood and gathered her personal belongings.

Mark, recovered from the sting, "I was hoping that you

would come back to Annapolis with me. Then we could go to New York together, and I could introduce you all. You don't even have their address."

"I've been in touch with Rose at work. They're going to meet me at the station."

Mark looked perturbed. Deflated, he replied, "They don't like me as you do."

Mary looked meaningfully at Mark and sighed. "Somehow, I was hoping that you'd say that you were sorry."

After a moment, she said, "I don't want to miss my train." She stood and prepared to leave. "Goodbye, Mark." Then she turned and walked away, leaving him sitting there alone.

Chapter 37
1938—New York City, New York

Mary stepped off the train at Grand Central Station and looked up one side of the platform, then looked in the other direction, and there was no one to meet her. She walked into the grand lobby and for the first few minutes after her arrival, it was teeming with passengers coming and going. When the crowd started to thin out, she looked around, but no Rose and Eddie were in sight

She walked over to the information counter. The clerk looked up. "May I help you?"

"I'm supposed to meet my brother and sister, but they're not here." She took out their photographs and showed them to the clerk. "I wonder if you can tell me if you have seen these two people today?"

"I'm sorry, Miss. We have so many people in and out of this station every day." The clerk looked at the photographs. "I'd like to help you, but I don't recall having seen them."

Mary tucked the photographs in her purse. "Thanks. I guess I'll just wait a bit."

She walked around the hall, amazed by its grandeur; the enormously high constellation ceiling, and the light streaming into the area through the exquisite arched leaded glass windows. She walked over to a bench to sit and wait. She looked up at the four-faced oval clock which stood in the center of the hall. The time was five p.m. An hour went by and she glanced at the clock. Disappointed, the tears started to fall. She wiped her eyes and gathered her belongings.

Mary walked outside and saw that it was raining. She reached for her umbrella and realized that she had left it in the station on the bench. She turned and walked back inside. After retrieving her umbrella, she turned to leave. Then her heart stopped.

At that moment she saw Rose and Eddie entering the lobby. Rose was lovely looking, with a trim figure. She had Gwen's beautiful auburn hair and she was dressed stylishly. Mary saw that Eddie was tall and a redhead. She thought that he was handsome and that he definitely looked just like Mark.

They approached Mary. Eddie called, "Mary?"

She was elated, "Yes?"

Rose waved, "It's us. Mary."

They appeared unsure of what to do next. It was a moment of wonder for each of them. They reached out and embraced each other awkwardly. Mary was choked up with emotion. Relieved, she said, "You weren't here. I wasn't sure what I'd do. Go to Bonwits, I guess."

Rose said, "But I don't work there anymore. I didn't get your letter until today when I picked up my final paycheck."

Mary said, "I'm sorry. It was really hasty of me to just come without waiting for an answer from you. I did have your home address from your last letter but, without thinking, I guess I automatically wrote to your work again."

Eddie said, "Here, let me take your bag, Mary." He picked up her suitcase and they left the station. He hailed a taxi and they headed towards Madison Avenue. They dropped her luggage at their apartment and went out on the streets of New York.

As they walked along the sidewalks, they made small talk about the city. Mary was walking on air. She was so ecstatic to be here in this wonderful, exciting city, and promenading along with her beloved brother and sister.

They strolled past the fancy windows on 5th Avenue. They walked past the Rainbow Room and Sardi's.

They stopped at the Horn and Hardart Automat in Times Square and took their dinner from the buffet counter. Being out and about town, Mary hadn't noticed that Rose and Eddie seemed reserved; but seated opposite them at the table, she thought that they were somewhat standoffish and she started to feel uncomfortable. She spilled her coffee, and hurriedly tried to clean it up. After a second coffee and dessert, they headed back to the apartment.

The apartment at 423 Madison Avenue was furnished simply, but even so, it was quite attractive. Rose was a very talented seamstress and the furniture, although vintage, had been made new with slipcovers created by her hand.

Mary and Rose were seated. Eddie carried a bottle of wine and three glasses. Eddie and Rose were still somewhat reserved in their interaction with Mary. She wasn't sure why.

"Do you drink wine, Mary?"

"Oh, yes. I'd love a glass."

They each took a glass and he poured.

He continued, "I apologize for our sparse furnishings. I'm sure you've been used to much more lavish accommodations."

She answered, "Are you kidding? I think it's all wonderful. And, the Beeler home was not grand by any means." She was feeling defensive and she didn't understand why. Now that she had partially come down off cloud nine, she noticed that they were speaking to her in a stiff manner; and only answering her questions in the least amount of words possible.

Then Eddie spoke very matter-of-fact. "What are your plans while you're here, Mary?"

Mary was taken back by his reserve. "Well, I guess I'll have to find a place to live. But, thankfully, I do have a job opportunity."

Rose asked, "Really? Where is that, Mary?"

"Through a fellow musician who moved to New York, I have an offer to play the piano in the Raleigh Room at The Warwick Hotel."

Rose said, "We didn't know you were a musician."

Then Eddie added, "But then, I guess there's a lot we don't know about you." They were silent again.

Mary said, "Have I done something to offend you?"

They were both quiet and looked at each other. After a moment, Rose spoke up, "We thought you were so wealthy that you didn't want any part of us."

Stunned, Mary answered, "How could you think that?"

Eddie spoke as though admonishing Mary. "Probably because we wrote to you many times, but, our letters were never answered."

Mary tried to explain, "I never got those letters. Mother Beeler kept them from me."

Eddie, not convinced, glossed over her response. He assumed an accusatory posture. "Why didn't you ever try to find us?"

"I never stopped trying to find you, but no one could tell me anything."

Mary said that she was so sorry that they thought that she didn't care to know them. She told them how desperately she had searched for them through the years. Then she said that the thought of finding them had sustained her in her darkest hours.

Rose asked, "How many years has it been since we were all together?"

Mary said, "Too many. I guess I was five years old, so it's been fifteen years."

Rose repeated slowly, "Fifteen years!"

They all sipped their wine, lost in thought.

Rose said that she remembered living in San Jose. "Our mother was an original." She shook her head. "She dispensed hugs, kisses, praise, fairy tales and absolutely no discipline. During that time, Eddie and I had roamed the orchards that covered San Jose for miles in every direction from the tiny little cottage in which we lived. We ran barefoot and never went to any school that I could remember. I think that Gwen was, in many ways, a free spirit. She was very proud of her beautiful auburn hair, part of her Irish blood, along with fierce independence and impulsiveness." Then she added that Gwen was also demonstrative, imaginative, and her own worst enemy.

Rose said that by the time she, herself, had arrived into this world, Gwen had already had a life that made any soap opera seem mild. Then she paused. "At that time, as became apparent later from what I knew of Gwen's story, we must have been very poor. But, we were never aware of that situation. Gwen would pick prunes in the orchards when she needed money or help like a field hand in the raisin drying benches. At some point, Gwen had become ill with kidney disease," but Rose said "I never realized it until I was about five. Then the signs of her illness started, and we left San Jose for her trek all over California to find a cure, mostly from faith healers and Chinese herb doctors."

Mary thought about how very sad it all sounded. She tried to think of the time when they were all together. It was the last time that she remembered being happy. "Do you remember running around on the dunes gathering sand verbenas for a bouquet for Mama?"

Eddie brightened. "That was when Mama worked at the Beach Cafe. I used to be the big brother in charge."

Mary said, "I remember when we all came into the cafe in the morning and had creamy coffee and apple pie. Do you remember that?"

Rose added, "Yes, and today that's still my very favorite breakfast."

Mary started to cry. "What the hell happened?"

Eddie spoke wistfully, "Mama became ill. She tried, but she just couldn't care for us all."

"But why me? Why did she give me away?"

"We were told that somebody wanted you, Mary. We thought that you were having a happy life."

Mary thought, *some life.*

Eddie told her, "When we fled to northern California, Gwen had no money and no job, so she would rent a place for us and then use credit to buy food. She enrolled me in whatever school was nearby. When it seemed that people were on to us, Gwen would move our little family in the middle of the night. I remember her saying that she made notes of what she bought and that she would repay her landlords and the shop owners when she was able. Then she would do the same thing in the next place.

This went on for a year or more. We were basically starving. I would go to school with no lunch, so I would go into the school library and read while my friends had their lunch, so they wouldn't notice. All the time, Gwen was contacting relatives to get their help, or for them to take her children so that they could be fed on a regular basis. But only you found a place."

And Mary thought, *oh yeah, some place.* And then she had felt so sorry for Rose and Eddie hearing about what they had been through in their young lives.

Eddie told her that he remembered their mother getting sick and very, very thin. One day, he came home from school and found her on the floor; his beloved mother.

He was only twelve years old. He said that he ran to the school and the rectory to tell the priest, but he was out of town. The only priest there spoke only Spanish, but he came with Eddie back to the house.

"The priest stood with me at the gravesite while I watched my dear mother being lowered into the ground and buried. Our beautiful mother was buried in a potter's field."

Mary shook her head. "How terrible that must have been for you. And, how very sad."

After a moment, she said. "If only I had seen your letters, it would have meant the world to me. And I would've wanted them more than anything."

Rose came to Mary and hugged her. "Oh, Mary. We're so sorry. We didn't know." She sat down next to Mary.

Eddie's demeanor softened. "Sorry, Mary. I don't know what we expected you to do. You were just a little girl." He took a seat across from the girls. "Did you know that Mama used to go to watch you on the playground when you were in grammar school? "

"She did? Oh my God! I think I could have suffered all the beatings I got, but I never could get over being left."

Rose answered, "Beatings?"

Mary sighed, "Oh, yes. God, it was all so terrible... being thrown away." She cried again.

Rose was teary. "Nobody asked to take us, so after Mama died, Eddie and I were both sent to a Catholic orphanage."

Eddie added, "And that was no picnic for either of us."

Rose told of her miserable childhood at the orphanage.

"There was one day," she said, "when I was quite young. I was hungry, so I went to the kitchen to find something to eat. I pulled a chair up to the counter and found a box of prunes in one of the cupboards. As I sat on the counter eating the prunes one of the nuns came in the room and found me. After reprimanding me, I was made to eat prunes until I puked."

Hearing this, Mary had shuddered.

Rose remembered that the sister in charge had been seemingly oblivious to what had been going on. They were not intentionally unkind, but ignorant of the needs of children. They were products of their narrow view of religion and the belief that life on earth was not intended to be happy. The children were told that they were to get their crowns in heaven after a hard, God-fearing life on this earth.

For weeks after she was dropped off at the orphanage, Rose said that she had waited every day for their step-father, Matt, to come to see her and take her out of there. She tried to get one of the sisters to send him a letter, but the nun insisted that her real father was dead. Every third Sunday was visiting day. She said that there was one of the washrooms with a window facing the front where visitors could be seen climbing up the hill. It was forbidden during the day to be anywhere but the established places, but she would risk any punishment to sit by that window and watch, hopefully. She said that anytime she would glimpse a large male figure, her heart would race in hope, but he never came and in time she knew that he must have moved on. She said that she still remembered him with love.

Instead, one day, the nuns told her that her father was there to see her, but when she ran to meet him, she screamed, "that's not my father." It was Henry Dierks who used to come to check on the children in honor of Guinevere. Then, Rose said, she ran to the upstairs window and watched him walk away, bent, limping and dejected. But, she said, I was only a little girl and I didn't understand the depth of his devotion to Gwen. Rose said that she never saw him again, but that he still sent his Christmas presents to her. Eddie said that he remembered Henry coming to visit Hansie during the years before the child died.

Mary told them that one day, she was out back at the Beeler's, picking lemons from the trees. She remembered that Mother Beeler had called to her saying, "Your father is here." But when she came into the room, there had stood an old man with a paralyzed face who looked as though he had had a stroke. She had cried, "He's not my father, he's not my father." Mary said that he tried to tell her that he had been to visit her brother, Eddie, and that he was so smart and had won many mathematical awards. But, she said that she wouldn't listen and that she ran out of there screaming, "It's not my father, it's not my father." And when he left, she got another whipping. It was not Mark, the father she remembered. It was Henry Dierks.

In later years they had learned that Henry Dierks who had lost everything and was living in a pauper's home in the Los Angeles area. He had been struck by a taxi and crippled and blinded in one eye. Every Christmas when the good women of the community would give him gifts, he would send them to Eddie and Rose in the orphanage. Then, even though he had no money for transportation, he found a way to go north to the San Francisco area to check on them.

Hearing this, Mary was deeply touched. She said that she now realized how devoted he was to Gwen and she wished she had been more mature and had been kind to him.

Eddie said that he was grateful to the Jesuits for his good education. They had seen that he was gifted and sent him to college. The same honor was given to Rose. She knew that she was one of only a few in the orphanage to be chosen to attend the area Catholic high school.

He told Mary that for one year in 1934, when Rose was sixteen, she left the orphanage and she and Eddie lived with Mrs. Olivia Fairbanks in Oakland, California. She was an older woman who had worked at the orphanage and had been nice to him through the years. At that point Eddie said that he had assumed the name of Fairbanks and dropped the name of Ellis, and Rose was encouraged to do the same. Then Rose had returned to the Orphanage for the next two years so that she might finish her education.

He was reflective for a moment. "After Mama died, the nuns contacted Mark. He sent back word that he had no children."

Mary spoke through her tears, "I know. I believe he has regrets."

Eddie added, "I'll never forgive that son-of-a-bitch. He abandoned our mother when she was so desperate, and he abandoned us."

Mary remembered Mark's words, "When I asked him what happened, he said that he had no choice."

Eddie said, "We always have a choice about the decisions we make in life. And now he expects us to care about him. Well, to bloody hell with him. We changed our last name long ago."

Rose added, "How could he be such an egotistical ass to think that after all that's happened, we would forgive and forget; that we would welcome him back into our lives?"

After a moment's reflection, Mary spoke, "Well, I am grateful to him for one thing. Despite his efforts to be in charge, he let slip where to find you."

Rose smiled, "Yes, we are grateful for that."

Eddie added, "For sure."

Rose turned and hugged Mary, and then Eddie came to embrace her.

Mary, filled with emotion, spoke. "It's taken fifteen years, but wouldn't Mama be thrilled to know that we had found each other. That we are all together again!" She paused a moment. "I would like to propose a toast." She raised her glass and Eddie and Rose raised their glasses. "To Mama, from her children who adored her."

All three in unison toasted, "To Mama."

That night they stayed up all night and talked. All night long, the story of their lives… and crying. If it is true that we can only be happy a few times in life then, despite the tears, that reunion was one of Mary's happiest times. She would remember, ever after, the joy she felt in that small room, in that apartment in New York.

THE END

Mary, Eddie and Rose at the New York World's Fair 1939

Epilogue

Mark and Helen were divorced in Switzerland in 1932. The marriage was short lived and surrounded by more mystery than her first marriage to Webster. When she left her fourth, and last, husband, Helen merely remarked that, 'another woman and some sort of lawsuit was responsible'.

After his divorce from Helen, Mark married her best friend, Rosa Josephine Centeno, the former Contessa Centeno.

Helen died March 28, 1935, in her Villa in Stressa Italy, but it was not until 1940 that her will went to probate. In a newspaper article headed:

BONANZA QUEEN LEAVES MORE THAN A MILLION, and subtitled, *SET UP TRUST FOR LAST HUSBAND*, it stated.

> *"Filing of the estimate disclosed that Mrs. Ellis had set up a trust fund for her last husband, Mark St. Clair Ellis, which at his death was to revert to the estate. Value of this, for the purpose of the estate, is fixed at $61,028.60 although the securities now in it are estimated to have a present (1940) value of $97,828.29."*

The property of Elizabeth Ellis, Mark's first wife, was valued at $35,000 in 1918 when she died. In 2018, the property would be valued at $862,834.

Commander Mark St. Clair Ellis died May 27, 1952. He is buried at Arlington National Cemetery.

Mary could never reconcile Mark's selfish behavior, nor his abandonment of Gwen and their children together, but once she found him, she wanted him to be a part of her life. She maintained a relationship with Mark until his death, and yet she recognized him for the total enigma that was his persona; brilliant, creative, but totally self-serving. Neither Eddie nor Rose chose to continue their association with Mark.

Henry Dierks, once prosperous, died a pauper on February 23, 1939. He had lived for many years in a home for the indigent in Los Angeles, California. He never lost sight of Gwen's children.

Through Gwen's generosity during her marriage to Henry Dierks, her sister Connie received an excellent education. She went on to become the Chief Librarian of the Navy Department in Washington D.C. Constance Evelyn Davies died January 30, 1957. She is buried at Arlington National Cemetery.

Guinevere Zepherina Davies died of complications of kidney disease on February 23, 1926, in Alameda County, California. She was buried in a pauper's grave with only a wooden cross for a marker.

When family members were asked why they neglected to come to Gwen's aid in her terrible time of need, all spoke of the unfavorable notoriety in the newspapers that had made their association difficult. So, it seems that Gwen was simply abandoned by everyone.

Edith and Gilbert Beeler remained a part of Mary's life. Somehow, Mary found a way to forgive Edith for her severe parenting. Even though she was a difficult woman and did not express affection often, Mary later realized that Edith did love her in her own way. Gilbert died early on, but Edith lived to age seventy-five. She died November 8, 1958.

Edward Mark Ellis Fairbanks, an engineer and inventor, received national acclaim in his twenties, when he built a Diesel style engine, and drove a car across the United States, operated solely on cooking oil. He later married and had two daughters. Eddie died July 4, 1996.

Rose Ellis Fairbanks graduated from Cornell School of Nursing with honors. She married a Commander in the Navy and had two daughters. Rose died April 1, 2004.

Mary Ellis Beeler, during her musical career of sixty years, received a Congressional Award for her contribution to the field of performing arts. She married and had six children, all of whom adored her. Mary died October 8, 1999.

Mary True at the piano